DON
DECEIVED

The definitive book on detecting deception

Mark McClish

Don't Be Deceived
The definitive book on detecting deception

Copyright 2012 by Mark McClish
ISBN 978-0-9679998-5-2

Published by
The Marpa Group, Inc.
P.O. Box 1478
Harrisburg, NC 28075

All rights reserved. No part of this publication may be reproduced without the prior permission of the publisher except for brief quotations and as provided by the United States copyright law.

Second printing 2013

Printed in the United States by Morris Publishing®
3212 East Highway 30
Kearney, NE 68847
1-800-650-7888

For more information on detecting deception, visit Mark McClish's web site at **www.StatementAnalysis.com**

Statement Analysis® is a registered trademark of Mark McClish

"The man of integrity walks securely, but he who takes crooked paths will be found out."

Proverbs 10:9

Contents

Introduction		7

Part One - The Language of a Liar
Verbal Statements — 11

Chapter 1	Words and Phrases	15
Chapter 2	Unique Words	31
Chapter 3	Extra Words	67
Chapter 4	Unusual Words and Phrases	73
Chapter 5	Pronouns	85
Chapter 6	Verb Tenses	103
Chapter 7	Words and Phrases That Indicate Untruthfulness	117
Chapter 8	Active Voice vs. Passive Voice	125
Chapter 9	Order Is Significant	131
Chapter 10	Personal Dictionary	141
Chapter 11	Emotions	161
Chapter 12	Words and Phrases That Span Time	169
Chapter 13	Articles	177
Chapter 14	Time References	183
Chapter 15	Did the Subject Answer the Specific Question?	191
Chapter 16	Did the Subject Answer the Question with a Question?	205

Contents

Part Two - The Language of a Liar
   Written Statements   217
      Chapter 17   Crossed Out Words   219
      Chapter 18   Story Breakdown   227
      Chapter 19   Punctuation   235

Part Three - The Actions of a Liar
   Nonverbal Communication   243
      Chapter 20   Hand Movements   245
      Chapter 21   Eye Movements   253
      Chapter 22   Leg Movements   259

Part Four - The Handwriting of a Liar
   Handwriting Analysis   265
      Chapter 23   Handwriting Traits   267

Final Thoughts   279

Notes   283

Introduction

It has been said that some people are good liars. These people usually possess the "gift of gab." They are smooth talkers who can convince you they are telling the truth. They use the right words and mannerisms to make their story sound believable. At the other end of the spectrum, there are people who are terrible liars. As soon as they knowingly tell a lie they feel ashamed for what they did. They may become flush and nervous. This may cause them to break eye contact with you showing you that something is not right. While there is no doubt that some people are better at hiding their deception, the truth is there are not very many good liars in the world. The reason people get away with lying is because we do not listen to what they are saying and we don't pay attention to what they are doing. If you know what deceptive signs to look for, you can greatly enhance your ability to spot a liar.

Law enforcement uses the latest technology in detecting deception. The polygraph records a person's blood pressure, breathing rate, pulse, and perspiration. The polygraph examiner will begin the test by asking the subject several questions he should be able to answer truthfully. This helps the polygraph examiner to establish a normal range for the subject. As the examiner asks questions concerning the investigation, he or she is looking for any changes in the subject's vital signs. A significant change such as a faster heart rate or an increase in the breathing rate indicates the subject is lying.

Voice Stress Analysis (VSA) uses a machine that measures human voice frequencies. The stress brought on by lying causes tremors in the vocal cords which changes the person's voice. While these changes are impossible to hear with the human ear the VSA can detect these micro-muscle tremors. When the machine senses the person is no longer speaking within his normal range it is an indication the person is lying.

Instruments such as the polygraph and the VSA are very useful tools. However, they are not very practical in every day conversations. Without the aid of a machine, there are only three ways you can determine if someone is lying. This can be done by examining how a person phrases his statement, by observing a person's body language, and by studying a person's handwriting. In this book, we will take a look at all three of these areas. Once you learn these easy to understand techniques you will be able to detect deception in any situation.

Part 1

The Language of a Liar

Verbal Statements

Verbal Statements

The English language is probably the most commonly spoken language in the world. This is because many non-English speaking countries teach English as a second language. While it may not be the most difficult language to learn it is full of paradoxes which can make it confusing even for a native speaker. We have words that sound alike but are spelled differently and have a different meaning such as *deer – dear* and *see – sea*. Then there are words that are spelled the same but have a different pronunciation and a different meaning. We *wind* our watches and we listen to the *wind* blow. A *minute* is a unit of measurement and something that is very small is *minute*. There are hundreds of these heteronyms in our language. Often times the English language sounds rather silly. We park our cars on driveways and drive on parkways. We call one of our favorite foods a hamburger even though it has no ham in it!

Despite its inconsistencies the linguistic richness of the English language allows a person to express himself in a variety of ways. Through the use of synonyms, slang, and a local vernacular there are usually several ways one can phrase a statement. What most people do not realize is they will always word their statement based on all their knowledge. Therefore, their statement may include information they did not want to reveal. Even though they may feel they are sharing very little information, people will provide you with more information than they realize. For habitually deceptive people, it can be difficult to separate the facts from the lies they are telling. However, at some point in their statement the truth will surface. This is because a person's true feelings will influence how he phrases his statement.

For the interviewer, much information can be obtained by examining the subject's language. Statement Analysis® is the process of analyzing a person's words to see if the person is being truthful or deceptive. These techniques will also reveal additional information within the person's statement. The Statement Analysis techniques are very accurate for three reasons.

First, the majority of the techniques are based on word definitions. Every word has a meaning. When you combine this with the fact that people mean exactly what they say, it then becomes possible to determine what a person is telling you and if the person is being truthful. If a person says, "I believe I will buy a new car" that is exactly what he means. He has not said that he will buy a new car. Therefore, you cannot picture him buying a new car. If a person arrested for a crime says, "I believe I will plead not guilty" we would have to question his innocence. An innocent person would be more definitive and say, "I am going to plead not guilty."

Secondly, some of the Statement Analysis techniques are based on the rules of grammar. For example, the rules of grammar define how articles are used in a statement. The indefinite articles "a" and "an" are used to identify someone or something that is unknown. Once the person or thing has been introduced, we are then required to use the definite article "the." Consider the following statement from an alleged robbery:

"I was standing at the bus stop when a man approached me and asked me what time it was. The man then pointed the gun at me and told me to give him my wallet."

In the first sentence, the victim properly refers to the attacker as "a man." Having identified the attacker, he then correctly refers to him as "the man" in the second sentence. A problem arises when he refers to the weapon as "the gun." Since this is the first time he mentions the weapon, he should have called it "a gun." Using the article "the" tells us the victim either recognized the gun or he is making up the story which was the case in this situation. Because he is thinking about placing a gun into his deceptive story, in his mind he has already made the introduction. Therefore, he uses an article that seems right to him but violates the rules of grammar.

The third reason why the Statement Analysis techniques are very accurate is because when applying the techniques you are not interpreting what the person is saying. No one can read someone else's mind. Instead, you are listening to what is being said. By paying close attention to every word spoken or written by the subject one can determine if the subject is being truthful. The key is to know what to look for in a statement.

Let's examine the language used by many liars. I will show you some things you should look for in a verbal and written statement to detect deception. People's words will betray them only if someone is listening.

Statement Analysis® is a registered trademark of Mark McClish

CHAPTER 1

Words and Phrases

It is very difficult to be a good liar. A person may spend hours thinking about how he is going to answer a question. He can consult with his attorney as to how he should craft his statement. Regardless of how much preparation is involved the truth will slip out. Let's look at some words and phrases that people have used which provided us with additional information and showed us they were being deceptive.

On March 25, 2002, Thomas Uzenski was serving as a detective with the Winterville Police Department in Winterville, North Carolina. While performing a routine on-foot survey of North Carolina Highway 11, Detective Uzenski found a pipe bomb in the ditch. Detective Uzenski got on his police radio and notified his chief who then called the North Carolina State Bureau of Investigation (SBI). The highway was immediately shut down and the bomb squad from the SBI determined that it was a live bomb and disarmed the device. The following day Detective Uzenski took agents from the Bureau of Alcohol, Tobacco, Firearms and Explosives (ATF) to the location where he had found the pipe bomb. To everyone's amazement, a second pipe bomb was discovered in the same area. The location had been thoroughly searched the day before when Detective

Uzenski found the first pipe bomb. Therefore, it was believed that during the night someone planted a second pipe bomb along the highway. The highway was again shut down and the second bomb was disarmed.

As the investigation into who planted the pipe bombs progressed, Detective Uzenski soon became the prime suspect. It was believed he planted the bombs and then pretended to find them in an effort to become a local hero. Detective Uzenski was charged with violating several provisions of the National Firearms Act and in 2003 went on trial in federal court in Greenville, North Carolina. Unlike most defendants, Detective Uzenski took the stand and testified in his own defense. In his testimony, twice he unknowingly admitted to planting these pipe bombs. Under direct questioning by his attorney, Detective Uzenski described finding the first pipe bomb.

"I back tracked and then as I was coming up towards the ditch I walked a little farther down, so I could come up around, as I came up on the ditch I was looking down on, it sort of sloped down and I noticed something shiny. So I stopped and it was little, it wasn't very level, so I braced myself, and I leaned down and I could just see a top part of, well, I just saw one part, I wasn't sure if it was a top part or whatever, so I reached down and I grabbed it, and then when I stood up and I looked closer at it, I realized what I had picked up."[1]

It was on a sunny day that Detective Uzenski found the pipe bomb. He told the jury that the sun's reflection off of the metal pipe caught his attention. He also unintentionally told the jury that before he picked it up he knew it was a pipe bomb lying in the ditch. We see his admission in his statement, "I leaned down and I could just see a top part of, well, I just saw one part, I wasn't sure if it was a top part or whatever."

Before he has a chance to thoroughly examine what he has found, Detective Uzenski testified he could see the "top part of." How did he know it was the top part? This indicates he already knew what was in the ditch. He realized what he had said and then tried to change his testimony, "well, I just saw one part, I wasn't sure if it was a top or whatever."

His second admission occurred under cross examination. The prosecution suggested that Detective Uzenski parked his car along the highway, got out and walked straight to the spot where he found the bomb. Detective Uzenski described walking around before finding the pipe bomb.

"I had covered approximately I'd say 30 to 40 yards already before I trekked back and recovered the first device."[2]

Did you see the confession? When a truthful person describes a past event he is relying upon his memory as he tells his story. It will be like a parade passing in front of him and he will state in sequential order everything that is occurring. He should be speaking from the perspective as if he is reliving the event. When Detective Uzenski stated that while on routine patrol he found the "first" device he was telling us that he knew there was or would be a second device. Some might say he used the word "first" because his memory was tainted. As he was testifying he knew there were two pipe bombs that had been found. That is possible but he should be telling his story as if he is experiencing it for the first time. None of this really matters because the true confession can be found with the word *recovered*. The word *recover* means to "regain" or "reclaim." That is exactly what Detective Uzenski did. He planted the pipe bomb the night before and the next day he reclaimed it. You might be thinking the use of the word *recovered* is cop talk. It is a term that is frequently used in law enforcement. However, it is always used to "regain" or "reclaim" something. If the police are searching for a drowning victim, upon finding the body they may state that they "recovered the body." Although they did not place the body in the water, they recovered it or reclaimed it for the family or for the community. The reason they would use the word *recovered* is because they knew what they were looking for. On the other hand, if you happened to find a body floating in the river, you would probably say that you "discovered a body" or you "found a body." You would use the word *discovered* or *found* because you were not expecting to find a body. Detective Uzenski did not discover the first device but instead he *recovered* it. He probably meant to say that he discovered or found the pipe bomb. However, he knows what the truth is and the truth came out without him realizing it. The prosecutor also did not realize or understand what Detective Uzenski had said and his statement was never used against him. Fortunately, ATF did a good job in gathering the evidence and Detective Uzenski was convicted of planting the pipe bombs.

In 1991, Bill Clinton was the governor of Arkansas and Paula Jones was an Arkansas state employee. Jones claims that on May 8, 1991 she was escorted by an Arkansas State Trooper to Governor Clinton's hotel room where the Governor propositioned her. Jones states that she refused the Governor's advances and left the room. In 1994, Jones filed a lawsuit against now President Clinton for sexual harassment. On January 17, 1998, the President testified at a deposition involving the lawsuit. In his testimony, President Clinton was questioned under oath about his relationship with White House intern Monica Lewinsky. It was believed the President was having an affair with the intern. If proven to be true, this could help bolster Jones's claim of sexual harassment. However, the President denied having a sexual relationship with Ms. Lewinsky. Jones's lawsuit was dismissed on the grounds that it had no merit.

Seven months later President Clinton would appear before a federal grand jury at the request of independent counsel Kenneth Starr. Starr was conducting several investigations including the Whitewater scandal, the firing of White House Travel Office personnel and perjury charges related to President Clinton's involvement with Monica Lewinsky. It was believed the President had lied under oath about his relationship with Ms. Lewinsky during his Paula Jones deposition earlier that year. As soon as the President took the oath to tell the truth at his grand jury appearance, Starr's team questioned the President about his understanding of the oath. They asked him if this was the same oath he took at his Paula Jones deposition. The President confirmed this was the same oath. After asking several more questions about the oath he had just taken, the President responded with this statement in regards to his Paula Jones deposition:

"I swore an oath to tell the truth, and I believed I was bound to be truthful and I tried to be."[3]

What does the word *tried* mean? It means "attempted." President Clinton told the independent counsel and the members of the grand jury that he was not completely truthful in his Paula Jones deposition. He tried to be truthful but he did not do it. A better statement would have been for the President to state that he "was truthful." Most people would agree that the President lied when he testified that he did not have a sexual relationship with Monica Lewinsky.

On July 19, 2004, Salt Lake City, Utah resident Mark Hacking reported that his wife Lori was missing. According to Hacking his wife left their house sometime between 5:30 a.m. and 6:00 a.m. to go for a jog in Memory Grove Park. Around 10:00 that morning, Hacking called Lori's office at Wells Fargo in Salt Lake City and found that his wife had not reported for work. At 10:49 a.m., Hacking called the police to report his wife was missing. When Lori's car was found near the park's entrance, the police immediately formed a search party comprised of law enforcement personnel and volunteers. While the search for Lori was underway Mark Hacking was talking to the news media. In one of his statements, he provides the following information:

> "It's hard because when I'm searching I'm not looking for somebody sitting on a rock or walking around. I know I'm searching for someone who is hurt."[4]

How does Mark Hacking "know" he is searching for someone who is hurt? No one else was talking that way. If Lori had been missing for a long period of time, there is a presumption that something bad may have happened to her. The problem is Mark Hacking made this statement the same day his wife disappeared. This is a clear indication he knew more than what he was telling the authorities. This is also an incriminating statement because he is telling us he has knowledge that his wife is hurt. Lori Hacking was not found that day. As the investigation into her whereabouts continued, the evidence indicated that her husband Mark was involved in her disappearance. On July 24, 2004, Mark Hacking admitted to his brothers that he shot Lori and placed her body in a dumpster. Shortly after his confession, Hacking was arrested for the murder of his wife. On October 1, 2004, Lori Hacking's body was found at the Salt Lake County landfill. On April 15, 2005, Mark Hacking pled guilty to killing his wife Lori. He told the judge that he shot Lori with a .22 rifle as she was sleeping. On the day he reported Lori missing, Hacking knew what happened to his wife. This caused him to say, "I know I'm searching for someone who is hurt."

On July 15, 2008, Orlando, Florida resident Casey Anthony reported that her three-year-old daughter Caylee was missing. As the police investigated the little girl's disappearance they knew that something was not right. Casey showed very little emotion and waited thirty-six days before reporting that Caylee had disappeared. Casey claimed that on June 9, 2008, she left Caylee with friend and nanny Zenaida Fernandez-Gonzalez. Casey said she lost contact with Zenaida and had not seen her daughter Caylee since June 9.

Casey told detectives that she worked at Universal Studios in Orlando and that there might be information in her office that could help in finding Caylee. On July 16, 2008, Casey and the detectives went to Universal Studios. After entering the building, Casey admitted to them that she did not work there. The detectives then interviewed Casey which produced the following questions and answers.

Detective: "Obviously I know and you know that everything you've told me is a lie. Correct?"
Casey: "Not everything that I've told you."

Several questions later:

Detective: "This has gone so far down hill and this has become such a mess.
Casey: Uh-huh (Affirmative)
Detective: We need to end it. It's very simple. We just need to end it."
Casey: "I agree with you. I have no clue where she is."
Detective: "Sure you do."
Casey: "If I knew, in any sense of where she was this wouldn't have happened at all."[5]

The detective stated that "everything" Casey has told him is a lie. Casey is able to deny this because she most likely did give some truthful information such as her name and address. However, her answer, "Not everything that I've told you" indicates that she has told some lies. Casey then stated that she has "no clue" where her daughter is. It is hard to believe that a person can honestly say that he or she has no clue or no idea about something. Most people have an idea on just about everything. I have an idea on how we could send astronauts to Mars. It probably would not work since I am not a rocket scientist but I do have an idea. Casey may not know where her daughter is but she should have a clue as to her whereabouts. She told the police she left Caylee with the Nanny. Wouldn't that be a clue? In her interview, she could have stated, "I agree with you, but I do not know where she is. The last time I saw her was when I left her with the nanny."

On that same day, Casey was arrested on suspicion of child neglect and obstructing a criminal investigation. While incarcerated at the Orange County Jail, Casey made a telephone call to her mother Cindy. The telephone call was recorded by the jail. In her conversation with her mother, Casey made the statement, "I have no clue where Caylee is."[6] Again we have Casey acting as if she has absolutely no information on the whereabouts of her daughter. This is a strong indication she is withholding information. On December 11, 2008, Caylee's body was found in the vicinity Casey's residence.

On May 24, 2011, Casey Anthony went on trial in Orlando, Florida for the murder of her daughter. During opening statements, Anthony's attorney, Jose Baez, told the jury that Caylee drowned on June 16, 2008 in the family pool. Casey Anthony panicked and did not call 911. This means Casey knew what happened to her daughter. This is why in July 2008 she said, "I have no clue" as opposed to saying "I don't know."

On July 5, 2011, the jury found Casey Anthony not guilty of first degree murder. They did find her guilty of providing false information to a law enforcement officer which is a misdemeanor charge. Many people were outraged with the jury's verdict believing the jury did not understand the meaning of reasonable doubt. The prosecution feels they tried the right suspect.

We saw the same language with Senator Joe Biden of Delaware. In August 2008 after Senator Barack Obama of Illinois received the Democratic nomination for the Presidency, Senator Biden was on the list of possible running mates with Senator Obama. On August 20, 2008, Senator Biden was asked by the press if he was going to be the Democratic Vice-Presidential candidate. He responded by saying, "I promise you I don't know anything. I have no idea."[7] I am sure Senator Biden did have an idea as he ended up becoming our nation's 47th Vice President.

On January 20, 2009, Barack Obama was sworn in as our nation's 44th President. With his inauguration, President Obama became the first African American to hold the office. The oath of office was administered by Chief Justice John Roberts. Justice Roberts strayed from the oath when he misplaced the word *faithfully*. The correct wording as prescribed by the Constitution is "I will faithfully execute the Office of the President of the United States." Justice Roberts stuck the word *faithfully* at the end of the sentence. Because Obama repeated Justice Roberts's flubbed words, many felt he should retake the oath to ensure he met the constitutional standard. On January 21, 2009, the CBS News reported, "White House press secretary Robert Gibbs says there are no plans for the president to retake the oath."[8] However, later that same day President Obama did retake the oath of office out of an abundance of caution. So, did CBS News get it wrong when they reported there were "no plans" for the president to retake the oath of office? The answer is no because the White House did not state the president would not retake the oath. They only said there were no "plans" for him to retake the oath. People change their plans all the time. If a person says, "I am not doing that" then he probably won't do it. However, if he says, "I don't plan to do that" he hasn't made a final decision as to what he will or will not do.

Al Gore used the same language when he was asked if he would run for President in 2008. The former Vice President stated, "I don't have any plans to be a candidate again."[9] It turned out he did not run for president. This was a good political answer because at the time it did not shut the door on a possible presidential run. In contrast, let's look at a statement made by Illinois Governor Rod Blagojevich who on December 9, 2008 was arrested by the FBI on federal corruption charges. It is believed that Governor Blagojevich attempted to sell Barack Obama's vacant U.S. Senate seat after Senator Obama became President Obama. After being released on bond, the governor made his first public comment since his arrest. Here is a portion of his statement.

> "Now I'm dying to answer these charges. I am dying to show you how innocent I am. And I want to assure everyone who's here and everyone who's listening that I intend to answer every allegation that comes my way. However, I intend to answer them in the appropriate forum, in a court of law. And when I do I am absolutely certain that I will be vindicated."[10]

The first thing we see is the governor is "dying" to answer the charges that have been brought against him. Although he may be dying he has not told us that he will answer the charges. We see further evidence he may avoid answering the charges when he says, "I intend to answer every allegation." The word *intend* means a person has in mind to do something. It does not mean the person will do it. People often have great intentions especially at the beginning of a new year to lose weight, get in shape, achieve better grades or make more money. Sometimes they fall short of obtaining their goal. Remember when sportscaster Marv Albert was charged with assault in 1997? He stated, "I categorically deny these charges and intend to vigorously defend myself against these allegations."[11] However, Marv Albert did not vigorously defend himself but instead pled guilty to charges stemming from the incident. A better statement by Governor Blagojevich would have been, "I will answer every allegation that comes my way."

The governor's statement, "I am absolutely certain that I will be vindicated" makes the governor sound very confident he will be exonerated. He uses the word *certain* to bolster his statement but it actually weakens the statement. The only way a person can use the word *certain* is if in his mind he is ruling out other possibilities which then leads him to conclude he is certain. The governor's own language tells us he has thought about the possibility of being found guilty. A person who has done nothing wrong probably would not contemplate a guilty verdict. A stronger statement would have been for the governor to say, "I will be vindicated."

On January 29, 2009, Governor Blagojevich was impeached and removed from office. On June 3, 2010, he went on trial in federal court in Chicago, Illinois charged with bribery, extortion, racketeering and a few other crimes. Although he had previously said, "I'm dying to answer these charges" and "I intend to answer every allegation" the governor chose not to testify at his own trial. He will probably say that his attorneys convinced him not to testify but his language told us that he was already considering not testifying. After deliberating for 14 days, the jury was deadlocked on all but one of the 24 charges against Governor Blagojevich. He was only convicted on the charge of lying to federal agents. The judge ordered a mistrial for the other counts. Some of the jurors reported they were deadlocked 11 - 1 in favor of convicting the governor on the more serious charges.

The following year government prosecutors retried Governor Blagojevich. On June 24, 2011, a jury found him guilty on 11 criminal counts related to President Barack Obama's old Senate seat and six counts involving fundraising shakedowns. On December 7, 2011, he was sentenced to 14 years in prison.

Charlie Crist is a former governor of Florida. He was elected as a Republican governor in 2006 after having served as a Florida State Senator, Education Commissioner, and Attorney General. Crist announced in 2009 that he would run for a seat in the United States Senate instead of running for re-election as the governor. Also running for the same senate seat was fellow Republican Marco Rubio the former Florida House Speaker. In March of 2010, the polls were showing Rubio with a comfortable lead over Crist for the upcoming August 24 primary. Speculation grew that Crist may switch parties and become an Independent in an effort to keep his name on the ballot for the November 2010 election.

On March 28, 2010, Crist appeared on the news show *Fox News Sunday* which was hosted by Chris Wallace. On the show, Crist stated, "I'm running as a Republican."[12] Wallace then asked Crist if he would support the winner of the GOP primary even if Marco Rubio won. Crist replied, "Of course I will, of course I will."[13] When people use the phrase *of course* they want you to take for granted what they are saying is the truth. Let's say you ask a friend if he will be attending a party you are hosting this weekend. He answers you by saying, "Of course I will be there." What he is saying is you should know he will be at the party. It is a given he will be there. The problem is we cannot assume anything. We can only believe what people tell us. If you tell me you will be at the party, then I can believe you will be there. If you tell me "Of course I will be at the party" then I have to believe you want me to take for granted you will be there. That means you may or may not attend the party. Crist's statement that he will "of course" support the winner of the GOP primary is weak.

As it turned out, Crist's words betrayed his intentions. One month later on April 29, 2010, Crist announced he was going to run as an Independent in an effort to win the Florida senate seat. On August 24, 2010, Marco Rubio won the Republican primary. Crist did not support Rubio even though he wanted us to believe he would support him. Instead, he ran against him as an Independent candidate for the same senate seat. In November 2010, Rubio won the Florida senate seat by a 19-point margin.

Over the past few years, steroid use in major league baseball has become a hot topic. While some players have admitted to using the performance enhancing drug, others such as pitcher

Roger Clemens have denied it. Brian McNamee, a former trainer who worked with the baseball great, claims that during Clemens's career he injected Clemens with performance enhancing drugs. McNamee's accusations are part of George Mitchell's report to Congress in December 2007 on steroid use in Major League Baseball. As part of Congress's investigation, on February 12, 2008, Andy Pettitte, a former teammate of Roger Clemens, stated in a sworn affidavit that Clemens told him nearly ten years ago that he used human growth hormone. On February 13, 2008, Roger Clemens testified in Washington, D.C. before the House of Representatives, Committee on Oversight and Government Reform. During his testimony Representative Elijah Cummings asked Clemens about Andy Pettitte's affidavit.

Cummings: "Now, Mr. Clemens, I remind you that you are under oath. Mr. Clemens, do you think Mr. Pettitte was lying when he told the committee that you admitted using human growth hormones?"

Clemens: "Mr. Congressman, Andy Pettitte is my friend. He will – he was my friend before this. He will be my friend after this. And again, I think Andy has misheard."

Cummings: "I am sorry, I didn't hear you?"

Clemens: "I believe Andy has misheard, Mr. Congressman, on his comments about myself using HGH, which never happened."[14]

Clemens says that Pettitte "misheard" their conversation about human growth hormones. However, Clemens qualifies his statements by using the words *think* and *believe*. These qualifying words show us that Clemens has a lack of conviction in what he is saying. We would expect Clemens to keep his statement short and to the point; "Andy Pettitte misheard me."

On July 13, 2011, Roger Clemens went on trial for lying to Congress about using performance enhancing drugs. On the second day of trial, the judge abruptly declared a mistrial after the government inadvertently allowed the jury to hear statements the judge had banned. Roger Clemens second trial is set to begin on April 17, 2012.

If you want to detect deception, you need to analyze a person's language. People's words will betray them. The truth will begin to surface. Ask yourself, "What is this person telling me based on the words he is using?" Remember that the information a person does not want to share with you will influence how he phrases his statement. Look for qualifying words that change the meaning of the statement. Ask yourself how you would phrase a statement and this may help you to see what the person is saying. The truth will come out. Sometimes it may be just one word. This is why it is important to pay close attention to every word spoken by the subject.

CHAPTER 2

Unique Words

In my research on deceptive language, I found there are several unique words deceptive people like to use. Some of these words are unique based on their definition. Others words are unique because they frequently appear in false statements. People will use these distinctive words without realizing their language is showing they are being deceptive.

Never

The word *never* means not ever. Since I have chosen to not jump out of a plane, I can correctly use the word *never* when I state, "I have never been skydiving." Because the word *never* is a negative word, deceptive people will sometimes use it as a replacement for the word *no*. However, the word *never* does not mean *no*. Therefore, you can not substitute the word *never* for the word *no*. Look at the following question and answer concerning a shooting.

Question: "Did you bring a gun to his house?"
Answer: "I never had a gun."

The answer sounds good because it is has a negative tone and if the person truly never possessed a gun, then he must not have had one when he went to the house. However, the question requires a *yes* or *no* answer. The subject has substituted the word *never* for the word *no*. This is an indication he did have a gun when he went to the house. It turned out the subject was lying and admitted that he brought a gun with him. It is hard for some people to directly tell a lie by using the word *no*. Therefore, they will resort to using the word *never*.

Ted Haggard is the founder and former pastor of the New Life Church in Colorado Springs, Colorado. On November 3, 2006, Haggard stepped down as the pastor of his church because of allegations made by Mike Jones, a former male prostitute. Jones claimed that for three years he engaged in sex with Haggard who went by the name Art. Shortly after Jones made his accusations Haggard was interviewed outside his home by television station KUSA 9NEWS in Denver, Colorado.

Reporter: "Have you had a relationship with –"
Haggard: "I have not."
Reporter: "Any kind of gay relationship –"
Haggard: "I –"
Reporter: "At all?"
Haggard: "I, I've never had a gay relationship with anybody and I, I'm steady with my wife. I'm faithful to my wife."[1]

The first thing we see is Haggard did not let the reporter finish the question. Before being interrupted, the reporter was able to ask, "Have you had a relationship with?" Haggard answered "I have not." Haggard denies a relationship but we do not know with whom he did not have a relationship. Haggard is guessing the reporter is going to ask about his accuser Mike

Jones. However, we cannot associate his denial with Mike Jones since his name was never mentioned in the question.

Haggard does the same thing again and starts to answer the second question before it is completely asked. Once the reporter is able to ask the complete question, "Any kind of gay relationship at all," Haggard answers, "I've never had a gay relationship." Haggard does not answer the question with a *no*. Instead he uses the unique word *never* as a substitute for the word *no*. This indicates he is being deceptive about whether or not he was involved in a gay relationship.

On November 5, 2006, a letter from Haggard was read to the congregation of the New Life Church in an attempt to explain what was going on in his life. In his letter, Haggard stated that he was guilty of sexual immorality. Several years later in January 2009, Haggard was interviewed by Larry King. Haggard admitted that his sexuality was confusing and that he still has thoughts about men "from time to time but not compelling thoughts."[2] It was also revealed on the show that a former male church member stated that several years ago he was in bed with Ted Haggard and Haggard masturbated in front of him. Haggard said the story was "fundamentally true."[3] Haggard also admitted that his preaching against homosexuality "was hypocritical."[4] That same month Haggard told Oprah Winfrey that he struggles with homosexual urges but insisted he is not gay. He said he has "sexual thoughts about men, but they're not compulsive anymore, and I do have temptations, but they're not compulsive."[5] Based on his statements in 2009, we can conclude that in 2006 Ted Haggard was being deceptive when he used the word *never*.

In March of 2006, Secretary of State Condoleezza Rice was asked if she would consider running for President in 2008. She gave the following answer.

> "I have never wanted to run for anything. I don't think I even ran for class anything when I was in school."[6]

Rice did not answer the question with a *yes* or *no*. Instead, she used the word *never* as a substitute for the word *no*. Rice is not necessarily being deceptive. Instead, she is giving a good political answer. If she would have answered "no," that would have dashed any hopes she may have had of becoming president. If she answered "yes," that would have caused a firestorm amongst the press. Therefore, Rice gave an answer in which she avoided committing herself. Her use of the word *never* tells us that she did indeed think about running for president. We do not know how much thought she gave to it but we do know it crossed her mind. Otherwise, she would have answered the question using the word *no*.

John Connolly is a former FBI agent who is currently in federal prison. Connolly grew up in South Boston in the same neighborhood where James "Whitey" Bulger's family resided. As adults Connolly would join the FBI and Bulger would join the Irish Mob. Because of his contacts with the Irish underworld, Connolly was able to convince Bulger to become an FBI informant. Bulger turned out to be a valuable asset providing information that helped Connolly and the FBI bring down Boston's Italian Mob. By dismantling the Italian Mafia, Connolly received numerous accolades and Bulger was able to build his criminal empire.

Connolly retired from the FBI in 1990. With Connolly gone, the FBI stopped using Bulger as an informant and instead turned their attention to his illegal activities. In 1995, charges were filed against Bulger and his associates for racketeering and extortion. The investigation also uncovered Connolly's secret deal with Bulger. In exchange for information, Connolly would tip Bulger off to any investigations that targeted his crew. Connolly also falsified reports to hide Bulger's crimes. In 1999, Connolly was indicted for alerting Bulger, falsifying reports and accepting bribes from Bulger. He was convicted in 2002 and sentenced to 10 years in federal prison. In 2005, he was indicted on murder and conspiracy to commit murder charges in the 1982 death of John Callahan. It was believed that Callahan was killed on Bulger's orders after Connolly told Bulger that Callahan was cooperating with the police who were investigating Bulger and his crew. In 2008, a jury convicted Connolly of second degree murder. He was sentenced to 40 years in prison.

Shortly after his arrest in 1999, *Dateline NBC* profiled John Connolly's case. Connolly was interviewed by correspondent Dennis Murphy. Murphy asked him about crossing the line that separates a good cop from a bad cop.

Murphy: "Did you go too far over the line?"
Connolly: "Anyone in my business, that knows what they're doing, knows enough to walk up to that line but never step over it."
Murphy: "And you didn't?"
Connolly: "I never stepped over that line."[7]

The first question Murphy asked Connolly requires a *yes* or *no* answer. Connolly chooses not to answer the question with a *yes* or *no*. In fact, Connolly does not answer the specific question. Instead of denying that he crossed the line, he states that "anyone" in his business knows not to step over the line. This is a truthful statement. The men and women in law enforcement know they should not cross the line that separates right from wrong. Murphy then basically asked Connolly the question again "And you didn't?" Instead of saying, "No, I didn't" Connolly uses the word *never* as a substitute for the word *no*. Even after being convicted of various crimes, Connolly maintains he is innocent. The evidence indicated he was guilty and so does his language.

In chapter one, we looked at a portion of Roger Clemens testimony before Congress in regards to his denial that he took performance enhancing drugs. When we look at more of his February 2008 testimony we find the following question and answer.

Question: "And let me ask just a general question. Did you during your playing career use steroids?"
Clemens: "I never used steroids. Never performance enhancing steroids."[8]

The question asked of Roger Clemens requires a *yes* or *no* answer. Clemens does not answer the question with a *no* but chooses to use the word *never* as a substitute for the word *no*. It appears he then qualifies his answer by stating he has never taken "performance enhancing" steroids. Does this mean he has taken steroids that did not enhance his performance? There are steroids such as epitestosterone which have not been shown to enhance athletic performance. However, epistestosterone can be used to mask a high level of testosterone. Therefore, it has been banned by many sporting authorities.

Remember that the word *never* means not ever. Therefore, if a person is asked, "Have you ever…?" it is acceptable for the person to respond, "I have never." By using the word *never*, he may be saying, "I have not ever done that" as opposed to using it as a substitute for the word *no*. We see an example of this when Governor Bill Clinton was running for President. While on the campaign trail in 1992, the soon to be elected President was asked about his drug usage.

Reporter: "Have you ever used illegal drugs?"
Clinton: "I have never broken the laws of my country."[9]

To the casual listener, the answer sounds good since illegal drug usage would be in violation of laws of the United States. A better listener may notice that Governor Clinton used the word *never* in his answer. Since the interviewer is seeking a *yes* or *no* answer, it could be deduced that Governor Clinton was substituting the word *never* for the word *no*. A well trained listener would realize that since the interviewer asked, "Have you ever" it is appropriate for Governor Clinton to respond, "I have never." However, a well trained listener would also examine the language used by Governor Clinton. He talks about not breaking the laws of "my country." Therefore, we can believe he has not broken the laws of the United States. But what about breaking the laws of another country? A perceptive reporter finally realized what the Governor was saying.

Governor Clinton was then asked if he had ever broken the laws of another country. Only then did he admit that while attending college in Oxford, England he experimented with marijuana.

If you want to detect deception, listen for the word *never*. The use of the word *never* can make a denial sound believable. Therefore, you should ask yourself if the person has used it correctly or has he used it as a substitute for the word *no*. If it is used in lieu of the word *no*, this is a weak denial because the word *never* does not mean *no*. There is a good chance the person has not answered the specific question. You should ask additional questions to get to the truth.

Actually

When people use the word *actually* they are comparing two thoughts. Consider the following question and answer.

Question: "Did you buy a new car?"
Answer: "Actually, I bought a new truck."

The person used the word *actually* in his answer because he was comparing buying a new car with buying a new truck. The interviewer asked if he bought a car and he responded that he bought a truck. The majority of the time when a person uses the word *actually* we can see what two things he is comparing. When we are uncertain of the comparison then we may have some undisclosed information. This occurs when the word *actually* is used even though nothing has been proffered by the interviewer as seen in the following exchange:

Question: "What did you do last night?"
Answer: "Actually, I went to the movies."

In this question, the interviewer has not suggested anything the person might have done. He simply asked him what he did last night. Therefore, the subject should have answered, "I went to the movies." The use of the word *actually* tells us the person is comparing going to the movies with something else. That something else is information the interviewer probably wants. The person may be thinking about something he wanted to do instead of going to the movies. Perhaps he wanted to stay home and watch television but his wife dragged him to the movies. Or, it could be that he did not go to the movies and he is thinking about what he did do that night. In either scenario, we have some undisclosed information that is brought to light by the use of the word *actually*.

On February 8, 2007, Anna Nicole Smith, a former Playboy Playmate and Guess model, was found unconscious at the Seminole Hard Rock Hotel and Casino in Hollywood, Florida. Paramedics rushed her to the hospital but she was pronounced dead on arrival. Her death was due to an overdose of prescription drugs. That same night Larry King interviewed Smith's sister Donna Hogan on his show *Larry King Live*.

King: "How, Donna, did you get the news today?"
Hogan: "Actually, I was tracked down by the media force and told. So that was really bad."[10]

Hogan uses the word *actually* which shows us she has some undisclosed information since King did not suggest how she received the news of her sister's death. She is comparing being tracked down by the media force with something else. She was probably thinking it would have been better if she had been notified by the authorities or family members rather than the press. She alludes to this when she says, "So that was really bad."

On June 12, 1994, Nicole Brown Simpson and her friend Ronald Goldman were brutally murdered at Nicole's home in Brentwood, California. Nicole was the ex-wife of former football great O.J. Simpson. As the police investigated the murders O.J. Simpson became the focal point and was arrested for the double homicide. Simpson was found not guilty of their murders in a 1995 criminal trial but was found liable for their deaths in a 1997 civil trial.

On January 15, 1998, O.J. Simpson was interviewed on ESPN's *Up Close* program. The question-and-answer format was hosted by Chris Myers. The topic of discussion was the death of Nicole Brown Simpson and her friend Ronald Goldman.

Myers: "Are you capable of killing somebody?"

Simpson: "You know I would say, actually I would say no, even though I'm sure if someone was presenting some imminent danger to my kids or something I'm sure everybody would be capable."[11]

When Simpson uses the word *actually* what is he comparing? He is comparing his answer of "no" to what? The opposite of *no* is *yes*. It would appear Simpson was about to say he was capable of killing someone but then used the word *actually* and changed his answer to *no*. He is being so guarded he does not want to admit he is capable of killing someone. Most people would acknowledge they could kill in self-defense. Simpson alludes to this when he talks about his kids but he does not personalize it. He does not tell us that he could kill someone in self-defense. Instead, he says he is sure "everybody" would be capable.

In the 2005 movie *Hitch*, Will Smith plays the role of Alex "Hitch" Hitchens a professional date doctor who teaches men the right things to say and do in order to get women to notice them. While interviewing one potential client, Hitch asked the man how he met the woman of his dreams. The man answered, "Actually, I was in a shop buying pajamas for my mom." The word *actually* tells us that in his mind the man is comparing buying pajamas for his mom with something else. Most men probably do not buy pajamas for their mother. Hitch saw through the man's deception and responded with, "And by that of course you mean you were buying lingerie for another woman?" The man then admitted that was indeed the case. Because the man was telling a lie, it caused him to use the word *actually*. Even though this is a fictional movie the Statement Analysis techniques still work. This is because the screenwriter knows who is lying and who is telling the truth. Therefore, the screenwriter will unknowingly have the person telling a lie answer the question just like a deceptive person would answer it. You can sometimes solve a murder mystery movie in the first fifteen minutes by analyzing the language.

In chapter one, I talked about Casey Anthony and the disappearance of her daughter Caylee. When Cindy Anthony realized her granddaughter was missing she called 911. She ended up making two phone calls to 911 the same day. During the second call the operator asked to speak to Casey.

911:	"Hi. What can you…can you tell me what's going on a little bit?"
Anthony:	"I'm sorry?"
911:	"Can you tell me a little bit what's going on?"
Anthony:	"My daughter's been missing for the last thirty-one days."
911:	"And you know who has her?"
Anthony:	"I know who has her. I've tried to contact her. I actually received a phone call today. Now from a number that is no longer in service. I did get to speak to my daughter for about a moment; about a minute."[12]

By using the word *actually*, Casey Anthony is comparing receiving a phone call with what? Receiving a phone call on another day? Not receiving a phone call? The defense stated that Caylee had drowned in the family pool. This means Caylee was dead when Anthony was speaking to the 911 operator. Therefore, Anthony could not have spoken to her daughter that same day. The most likely scenario is that Anthony did not receive a phone call from the nanny that day. Therefore, she unknowingly used the word *actually* because she was comparing not receiving a phone call with her lie stating that she did receive a phone call. She uses the word *actually* to bolster her statement but instead it weakens her statement and shows us she is being deceptive.

Financier Bernard Madoff is responsible for the largest investor fraud committed by a single person. His Ponzi scheme defrauded investors of nearly $65 billion. On March 12, 2009, Madoff pled guilty to charges that included perjury, fraud, and money-laundering. During his hearing Madoff offered the following apology.

> "I am actually grateful for this opportunity to publicly comment about my crimes, for which I am deeply sorry and ashamed."[13]

The question is how grateful is Bernard Madoff? A stronger and more sincere statement would be, "I am grateful for this opportunity." Since he used the word *actually*, we have to wonder what Madoff is comparing. He could be comparing having an opportunity to talk with not having an opportunity. He could also be comparing being grateful with not being grateful. We do not know if he is thinking that others may feel he is not grateful or if part of him is not grateful. This is similar to your boss complementing you by saying, "Actually, you did a good job." That is not a great compliment since his language tells you he thought there was a chance you would mess things up!

If you want to detect deception, pay attention to the word *actually*. People have the tendency to use it when they are thinking about something else. In most cases, you will be able to determine what the subject is comparing. If you do not see the comparison, this means the subject is thinking about something that he has not disclosed. He may be thinking about something he wanted to do or he may be thinking about something that he did do. You should inquire as to what is on his mind.

With

The word *with* in any sentence represents distance. When you see this word you will see something mentioned before the word and something mentioned after the word; the word *with* keeps them apart. People will sometimes reveal their true feelings when they use this word.

One Christmas season I asked a friend what he did over the weekend. He replied, "I went Christmas shopping with my wife." I told my friend that he did not want to go shopping and he confirmed my suspicion. The reason I knew he was dragged along on that Christmas shopping spree is because he used the unique word *with*. Look again at his statement: "I went Christmas shopping with my wife." Look at where the words "I" and "wife" are located within the sentence. They are as far away as you can get! Because he did not want to go shopping, he unknowingly placed himself at the beginning of the sentence and his wife at the end of the sentence. Had he said, "My wife and I went Christmas shopping," that would be a whole different meaning. In that sentence, the words *wife* and *I* are right next to each other. The word *and* connects the two of them. This would indicate he is a willing participant. When I asked my friend what he did over the weekend he did not think about how he should phrase his answer. He simply answered the question based on how he felt. The information that a person does not want to share will influence how he phrases his statement.

I once analyzed a statement written by a husband whose wife died in an automobile accident. The husband stated that he and his wife were in their car driving to a restaurant to get breakfast.

He was driving and she was seated in the passenger seat. Before they arrived at their destination, he had to go to the bathroom. He pulled his car over onto the side of the road and got out to relieve himself in the bushes. The only problem was he did not turn off the car's engine and he forgot to put the car in park. Once he stepped out of the vehicle it continued to move forward and went over a cliff into a ravine. His wife was killed in this so-called accident.

When I looked at his statement I noticed a problem with the very first sentence. The husband wrote, "That on Saturday morning I was with my wife Cathy and we were going to have breakfast in Jacksonville." The husband created distance between himself and his wife by using the word *with*. We would expect him to say, "Cathy and I were going to breakfast." By using the word *with*, he was unknowingly telling us there was a problem with their relationship. It does not mean he was going to kill her. It does not mean they were going to get a divorce. However, his language absolutely means there was some discontent that morning. This is an important clue when we are investigating a suspicious accident that resulted in a death. As I continued to read his statement I saw other signs of deception that made it very clear this was no accident. The husband purposefully did not put the car in park and exited the vehicle allowing it to roll over the cliff. The jury also saw through his deception.

Another tell-tale use of the unique word *with* occurs when a person lies about what he was doing at a given time. For example, if a burglary suspect is asked to account for what he was doing during the time of the robbery, he may state in his alibi, "I was bowling with Joe." Since he did not go bowling but instead was committing the crime, it is difficult for him to say, "Joe and I were bowling." He cannot personalize his statement and show closeness to Joe and the bowling alley because he knows it is a lie. Therefore, he unknowingly uses the word *with* and distances himself from Joe. As I have already mentioned, information that a person does not want to share will influence how he phrases his statement without him realizing it. Even if witnesses confirm that the suspect and Joe were bowling, we still have a problem because of the word *with*. Why did he use the word *with*? Did Joe drag him to the bowling alley? The answer may be that he did go bowling but at some point in time he left the bowling alley and committed the robbery. He then returned to the bowling alley and resumed bowling hoping to solidify his alibi. Because he took a break from bowling this caused him to use the word *with*.

We see a similar use of the word *with* when telling a lie in the JonBenet Ramsey case. On December 26, 1996, the body of six-year-old JonBenet Ramsey was found in the basement of her home in Boulder, Colorado. The cause of death was strangulation with a garrote coupled with a skull fracture. The police conducted an extensive investigation which included scrutinizing her parents John and Patsy Ramsey. While many people have been cleared as suspects, to this day no one has been convicted of her murder.

The police thought they had a break in the case when John Mark Karr was arrested in Bangkok, Thailand on August 16, 2006. Karr was wanted in Sonoma County, California on child pornography charges. He was also wanted for questioning in the murder of JonBenet. For several years, Karr had been exchanging emails with a journalism professor at the University of Colorado. Based on the content of Karr's emails, it was apparent he was obsessed with JonBenet and her death. Since he was wanted for child pornography, he became a person of interest in JonBenet's death.

While detained in Bangkok, Karr was giving statements about the JonBenet case that many people interpreted as being a confession. In one statement to the press, he said, "I was with JonBenet when she died; her death was an accident."[14] While this statement certainly implicates Karr was involved in JonBenet's death, it is not a confession. Karr never states that he killed JonBenet or caused her death. All he said was he was present when she died and her death was a mistake. On August 20, 2006, Karr was extradited to the United States. Eight days later the Boulder County District Attorney's Office announced that Karr was no longer a suspect when it was discovered that his DNA did not match the DNA left at the crime scene.

When we look closer at the statement made by Karr alluding that he was involved in JonBenet's death, we see he used the word *with*. He stated, "I was with JonBenet when she died." Why does Karr, who is infatuated with JonBenet, put distance between himself and her? One might think this is because he does not want to be associated with her death. The only problem is Karr was making numerous indirect references to being responsible for JonBenet's death. The reason he used the word *with* is because it is hard for a person to tell a direct lie such as "I killed JonBenet." It is much easier for a deceptive person to imply involvement or in most cases imply he was not involved.

Because Karr would not directly admit he killed JonBenet and because he was lying about his participation in her death it forced him to use the word *with*. This is an unusual case in which an innocent suspect lied about his involvement in a murder, but the Statement Analysis principle regarding the word *with* is still applicable. Karr may be guilty of obsession and psychosis, but he was not guilty of JonBenet Ramsey's murder.

I once watched an interview of a man who was babysitting a five-month-old baby. The baby was brought to the hospital with a skull fracture. The doctor on call was suspicious as to how the baby could have suffered such a severe injury. The police were contacted and discovered the man who was watching the baby was an ex-convict who was on parole. During their interview with the parolee we find the following exchange.

Police: "Tell me what you can about what happened."
Parolee: "I was playing with the baby. She fell asleep. I put her on the couch and made sure she was safe. Then I went to the bathroom and then I was there maybe 10 between 10 to 15 minutes and when I came back out she was screaming. She fell off the couch."

The subject uses the unique word *with* in the first sentence when he states, "I was playing with the baby." He could have stated, "The baby and I were playing on the couch." Why does he create distance between himself and the baby? This would be an indication the baby had already been injured at this point in his story. He does not want to take possession of an injured baby so he distances himself from the baby. Eventually the man confessed that he was smoking a joint and the baby was crying. He picked up the baby and while spanking her she fell out of his arms and hit the floor head first causing her injuries.

If you want to detect deception, you need to take note of the word *with*. Look to see if the person has used the word appropriately. The use of the word *with* does not always mean the person is being untruthful. One can show distance in a statement and still be speaking the truth. However, there are times when a person may unknowingly reveal his true feelings by using the word *with*.

Standing – Sitting – Laying – Lying

In my studies, I have found that when a person uses the words *standing*, *sitting*, *laying*, and *lying* to describe an inanimate object, it indicates the person is tense and possibly being deceptive. This is because these words are action verbs and non-living things are not capable of performing these acts.

There was a case in which the police received a tip there were illegal drugs in a residence. When the authorities entered the house they found a bag of marijuana on the dining room table. The two people in the house, Bob the owner of the house and John a visiting friend, were arrested for possession of marijuana. When the police questioned them about the marijuana, John denied it was his and gave a statement which included the sentence, "When I arrived at Bob's house I saw a bag of drugs sitting on the table." In trying to say the drugs belong to Bob, we see that John used the word *sitting* in referring to the drugs. Drugs are not capable of sitting. It turned out that John brought the marijuana to Bob's house. He did not want to admit to bringing the drugs so he claimed they were there when he arrived. Instead of saying the "drugs were on the table" he, perhaps unknowingly, chose to say they were "sitting on the table." The word *sitting* is an action verb. John used the word *sitting* because he was the one who was providing the action by placing the drugs on the table. If the drugs were already at the house and John performed no acts in regards to the drugs, there is a good chance he would not have used the word *sitting*.

In 1995, Jim Barton was a lieutenant with the Springboro, Ohio Police Department. On April 11, 1995, Barton returned home and found his wife Vickie had been murdered execution style with three gunshot wounds to the head. The case went unsolved until 1998 when the police got a break. A career criminal named Gary Henson told them that his half-brother William Phelps killed Vickie Barton. According to Henson, Phelps and an unknown accomplice burglarized the Barton home. During the robbery Phelps panicked and shot Vickie Barton. Four months after Vickie was killed, Phelps committed suicide. Because Henson knew details of the crime that had not been released to the public his story sounded believable. However, DNA evidence found at the crime scene did not match William Phelps. Therefore, the case remained opened as to who killed Vickie Barton.

In 2003, a cold case team took another look at Vickie Barton's murder. Within six weeks they found something that had been overlooked. When Jim Barton found his wife had been shot to death he called 911. On the 911 tape, Barton can be heard talking to himself. It sounded as if he said, "I gotta call Phelp man." This appeared to tie Barton with William Phelps. Barton would claim the 911 operator was not helping him and that he slurred his words and said "I gotta call fo-help man." Convinced that he said "Phelp," the cold case team re-interviewed Gary Henson who provided police with additional information. Henson now claimed that Barton hired Phelps to stage a burglary at Barton's residence and to scare his wife Vickie. It was known that Barton wanted to become the Police Chief and there was an unwritten rule that the Chief should reside within the city limits. Since Barton lived outside the city limits, the police theorized Barton wanted his wife scared into moving into a safer neighborhood in town.

In April 2004, Jim Barton was arrested for causing his wife's death. His trial began on February 7, 2005. Eleven days later the jury found him guilty of involuntary manslaughter and aggravated burglary. Barton was sentenced to 15 to 50 years in prison.

Peter Van Sant with the CBS News interviewed Barton for the show *48 Hours Mystery* which aired on October 29, 2005. In his interview, Barton described coming home that dreadful day.

> "I pulled down our farm lane. The garage door was standing open and the interior door was standing open as well. This seemed a little bit odd."[15]

Barton describes two doors leading into his residence as "standing open." Doors are not capable of standing. The use of the word *standing* indicates Barton may have been experiencing some tension. If Barton hired someone to burglarize his house and scare his wife, this would explain why he was tense as he approached his home. Barton stated that seeing the doors opened, "seemed a little bit odd." This could account for the tension but recognize that he downplays this. He said that this was only a "little bit" odd.

We see a similar use of the word *standing* with a delivery driver who said that he was robbed while driving his truck route. The armed robbers blocked his truck so he could not move and stole his cargo. In describing the robbery, the driver gave the following statement.

"I loaded my truck and left the store. When I stopped at Spring Avenue and 5th street I was assaulted by three men with weapons. Earlier in the day I saw a truck parked at Spring Avenue and 5th street. As I left the store I saw the same truck standing in front of me preventing me from passing. When I tried to pass the truck two men opened the door to my truck and pointed their weapons at me."

Just like with doors, trucks do not have the ability to stand. If we were interviewing this alleged victim, we would want to find out why he used the word *standing*. No doubt being robbed is going to cause some tension but most truthful people are not going to refer to the truck as "standing in front of me." Most people would probably have stated that the truck was "parked" in front of them. It turned out he was robbed but it was an inside job and the driver was a willing participant.

If you want to detect deception, you should listen for the words *standing*, *sitting*, *laying*, and *lying*. See if they are being used correctly or if they are being applied to a lifeless object. These are all action words meaning somebody performed the action since the object is not capable of doing so. It may be the interviewee carried out the action or he knows who did it. You do have to take into consideration that for some people the use of these words in regard to an inanimate object is part of their vernacular. Regardless, you still need to recognize that these words can provide important clues so when you hear them try to determine why the person used such language.

This – That – These – Those

The words *this* and *these* indicate closeness. The words *that* and *those* indicate distance. Let's say you and your friend Tim go to a party together. At the party, your friend John walks up to you. Tim and John do not know each other. Being a polite person you introduce them to each other. In doing so, you might say something like "Tim this is John." You would use the word *this* because John is standing in front of you. He is close by. Also at the party is Mike. You know Mike but your friend Tim has never met him. Mike is on the other side of the room. In pointing Mike out to Tim, you might say "Tim that is Mike over there." You would use the word *that* because Mike is some distance away from you. The same rule applies when we use the words *these* and *those* when talking about more than one thing.

In a truthful statement, these words are normally used correctly. However, in a deceptive statement, a person may forget which of these words he should be using. His choice of words may show his statement is bogus. Consider the following statement about an attack:

"As I was walking to my car this man appeared out of nowhere and hit me in the back of the head."

The victim referred to the attacker as "this man." Why does he use a word that shows closeness to the attacker? It is true the attacker was in close proximity to the victim. It is true he could be using the word *this* to single out the man. However, it is also true the word *this* indicates closeness. Most truthful people would probably say "a man appeared out of nowhere." We see the same thing in part of a statement given by a man who said he was robbed while he was answering nature's call in an alley.

"I was in the alley taking a leak when a man stuck a gun in my back. This person told me not to move. He started going through my pockets and found my money."

The man showed closeness to the robber when he referred to him as "this person." Most people would say "the man" or use the pronoun *he*. We see further signs of deception with the word *started*. The word *started* means the act was interrupted and perhaps not completed. This seems to contradict the idea the robber reached into his pockets and took his money. Most truthful people would state, "The man went through my pockets." This is a declarative statement that lets us know what happened. The statement, "This person started going through my pockets" leaves us to wonder if he finished going through his pockets.

On March 2, 1998, Jefferson Parish, Louisiana resident Patrick Kennedy claimed that he heard his eight-year-old stepdaughter screaming outside. He ran out of his house and found his stepdaughter in the side yard. She told him that two boys had raped her. Kennedy claims he saw one of the boys riding away on a blue 10-speed bicycle. Kennedy carried his stepdaughter into his house and called 911 to report the rape.

> "I need an ambulance. I need police. My little girl is eight-years-old. She was off in the yard and she said two boys grabbed her and raped my child and I'm trying to find these mother fuckers because I am going to kill them."[16]

When a deputy from the Jefferson Parish Sheriff's Office arrived at Kennedy's residence, Kennedy told the deputy that two boys dragged his stepdaughter out of their garage and to a side yard where they raped her. The deputy quickly realized that things were not adding up. Further investigation revealed that Kennedy called a carpet cleaning company two hours before his 911 call and asked how he could clean and remove blood stains from a carpet. Although the victim initially stated she was raped by two boys, she eventually confided to her mother that Kennedy was the one who raped her. Kennedy was charged and convicted of aggravated rape and was sentenced to death. Under Louisiana law, a person convicted of sexually assaulting a child under the age of 12 can receive the death penalty. The U.S. Supreme Court would eventually rule that states cannot punish the crime of rape of a child with the death penalty. Kennedy was then re-sentenced to life in prison.

Even before the police arrived at his house Kennedy was showing signs of being deceptive. In his 911 call, Kennedy stated he was going to try and find "these mother fuckers." By using the word *these* Kennedy was unconsciously connecting himself to the rapists. This does not make sense. Most truthful people would use the word *those*. Kennedy used a word that indicates closeness because he was making up the story. Since the men did not exist, it was easy for him to use language that connects him to the rapists.

If a deceptive person is going to misuse these words, he will probably misuse the word *this* to show nearness when there should not be such closeness. However, how a person uses the word *that* can also provide us with additional information. In talking about the unique word *with*, I mentioned the case in which a husband said his car accidentally went over a cliff killing his wife who was in the car. The husband began his statement saying, "That on Saturday morning I was with my wife Cathy and we were going to have breakfast in Jacksonville." The use of the word *with* showed distance between the man and his wife. We also see he used the word *that* to begin his statement. Most people would probably say, "On Saturday morning..." By using the word *that*, he is creating some distance between himself and what? He may be distancing himself from the day his wife died. This would be a natural reaction, but he could also be distancing himself from his statement. He knows that he purposefully killed his wife. He knows the statement he is about to give is not the complete truth. Therefore, this causes him to unknowingly begin his statement with the word *that*. If the only sign of deception was the strange use of the word *that*, we would have to conclude the statement is truthful. However, in this man's statement there were several indications he was being deceptive which included his use of the word *that*.

If you want to detect deception, listen to how a person uses the words *this*, *these*, *that* and *those*. It is true the words *this* and *these* indicate specificity. However, they also show closeness. Does it make sense that a person would show closeness at this point in his statement? Often times, a deceptive person will use the word *this* and place himself in close proximity to someone or something he should not be near. The misuse of the words *that* and *those* can also show if a person is not being completely truthful.

Three

Over the years, I have noticed that when deceptive people have to come up with a number they will often choose the number *three*. I am not sure why this is. Perhaps it is because we were unknowingly saturated with this number during our childhood. There are many fairy tales, novels and nursery rhymes that draw on the number *three*: The Three Little Pigs, Goldilocks and the Three Bears, The Three Musketeers, Three Blind Mice, Three Billy Goats Gruf. Then there are fairy tales that make subtle use of the number *three*. In Jack and the Bean Stalk, Jack climbs the beanstalk three times. Cinderella makes three visits to the ball. Rumpelstiltskin spun straw into gold three times and gave the queen three days to guess his name. In the original Brother's Grimm version of Snow White and the Seven Dwarfs, the queen tries to kill Snow White three times. Lastly, everyone knows if you rub the magic lamp the Genie will grant your three wishes. All of these references to the number *three* occur in fictitious tales. It may be that because of our upbringing we have associated the number *three* with untruthful stories and have unknowingly embedded this into our psyche. When we have to make up a number the number *three* often enters into our mind.

If the number *three* appears in a statement, it is an indication there may be deception in the story. Some examples of the deceptive three are: "Three men attacked me." "I left the house at 3:00." "I had $300 in my purse." It does not matter how it is used. If there is a reference to the number *three*, it is a sign the person may be lying.

Brian Wells was an employee of the Mama Mia Pizzeria in Erie, Pennsylvania. On the afternoon of August 28, 2003, he left the restaurant to deliver two pizzas. The next time Wells was seen he was robbing a PNC bank. As Wells exited the bank he was confronted by the police. When the police moved in to arrest him they discovered he had a bomb locked around his neck. Wells told the police that "three black men"[17] placed the bomb around his neck, started the timer and forced him to rob the bank. The police then backed off and called for the bomb squad. Unfortunately, before the bomb could be removed it detonated killing Brian Wells.

The case went unsolved until July 2007 when the U.S. Attorney's Office alleged that Wells was involved in the planning of the botched crime. Two co-conspirators were indicted by a federal grand jury on charges of bank robbery. A third suspect died of cancer in 2004 and a fourth suspect was given immunity. Counting Wells, it is believed there were five co-conspirators involved in this crime. None of them were black. When the co-conspirators decided to come up with a number of alleged hostage takers in the event Wells was caught robbing the bank, the number they chose to use was the number three. Wells could have told the police that two or four men made him to rob the bank. However, since he and his co-conspirators knew this was a lie, three is the number they decided to use.

I recently watched the movie *The Sentinel* staring Michael Douglas and Kiefer Sutherland. Douglas is a Secret Service agent looking for his informant, Walter Miller, who does not want to be found. In an effort to find Miller, Douglas poses as a representative of the Publishers Clearing House. He goes to Miller's mother's residence and tells her that her son has won some money. She tells Douglas, "I don't know where he is. Walter and me haven't spoken in three years." As soon as Douglas leaves her house the mother calls her son to alert him the police are looking for him. As I mentioned earlier, even though this is a fictional movie the writers know the mother is supposed to lie to Douglas. So, when writing the script the writers unknowingly have the mother use deceptive language. They could have had the mother state she has not spoken to her son in one year, two years, or even four years, but the number they chose was *three*.

We see the same thing in the television show *LOST*. The show, which ended with its sixth season in 2010, was about a commercial airliner that crashed onto an uncharted mysterious island. The survivors of the crash discover there are other people living on the island who are not very friendly. The survivors refer to these original inhabitants as "The Others." In a season two episode entitled "One of Them," a man is caught in a trap set by a friendly inhabitant named Danielle Rousseau. The trap involved a trip wire and a cargo net that engulfed the man and hoisted him up into the air. Rousseau brings Sayid, one of the survivors, to the stranger. Rousseau suggests that he is one of "The Others." The man replies, "I have no idea what she's talking about." The phrase, "I have no idea" is our first indication the man is being deceptive. Sayid releases the man from the trap and asked him who he is. He tells Sayid that his name is Henry Gale. He said that he and his wife were traveling in a hot air balloon and crashed onto the island several months ago. His wife became sick and died "three weeks ago." The number *three* is our second clue this man is being deceptive. The survivors take the man into custody but he soon escapes. It turned out this mysterious stranger was Benjamin Linus; he was the leader of "The Others." The writers for the show *LOST* could have picked any number they wanted to when referring to how long ago the man's wife had died. He could have told Sayid and Rousseau that it was one week, two weeks, or months ago that she died. However, since he is supposed to be lying, the number the writers chose without realizing it was the number *three*.

Deceptive language would continue to appear throughout the show. One of the survivors, Jack, is a spinal surgeon. In the season three episode, "Every Man for Himself," Jack sees an x-ray of a spine that has a tumor. Jack speculates the x-ray belongs to Benjamin Linus. Jack asks Ben if the tumor has caused a tingling sensation in his fingers. Ben responds, "I have no idea what you are talking about." Eventually, Ben admits the x-ray belongs to him and Jack performs surgery to remove the tumor.

Later on in season three in the episode "Not in Portland," the survivors are trying to find a friend who they believe is being held captive by "The Others." The survivors overtake a guard standing post outside of an unknown building. When they ask the guard where their friend is he replies, "I have no idea." Once they threaten to shoot him in the knee he tells them their friend is inside the building.

Let's get back to the number *three*. I once received an email that had a return address of office@fbi.gov. At the time, I was a Deputy U.S. Marshal and it was not unusual to receive an email from an FBI agent, but it seemed odd the FBI would send an email to my home email address. It seemed even stranger when the email stated, "A monitoring of your IP address shows that you have visited illegal websites more than 30 times." I checked on the internet and found this was indeed a bogus email. The email had an attachment that contained a virus. Common sense told me this was probably a phony email and so did the number *30*. The person who wrote this email could have chosen any number. Since he knew this was a fake email, this caused him to unknowingly use the number *30*.

When we looked at the unique word *standing*, I talked about the delivery driver who claimed he was robbed. One indication there was something wrong with his story is that he referred to the truck as "standing in front of me" and not allowing him to pass. Another sign there was deception in his story is that he stated he was assaulted by "three men." As I had mentioned it was an inside job and he was involved in the robbery.

On January 14, 2010, Brandon Lockett of Roanoke, Virginia reported that three men broke into his apartment and knocked him unconscious. Lockett claimed that when he woke up he found his four-year-old stepdaughter tied up and his two-year-old stepson Aveion Malik Lewis was gone. A ransom note was left behind demanding $10,000 for Aveion's return. An Amber Alert was issued and the police gave a description of the men and the vehicle they may be driving.

The police were suspicious of Lockett's story about the kidnapping. Several days later, they brought him in for questioning. It was then that Lockett confessed to the police that Aveion was dead before he made the 911 call. However, Lockett refused to give any details on the boy's death or the whereabouts of his body. When Lockett fabricated the story about Aveion being abducted, the number of kidnappers he chose for his story was three. On January 27, 2010, Aveion Lewis's body was found at the Roanoke landfill. Brandon Lockett and his wife Morgan Elizabeth Ward Lockett were charged with second-degree murder, child neglect and cruelty.

There is one exception to the number three rule. When a person is stopped for suspicion of driving under the influence the police will often ask the driver how many drinks he had. Many deceptive people will respond, "I only had two drinks officer." In some cases, it may sound like this; "I only had two drinks, occifer!" When it involves alcohol, *two* seems to be the standard deceptive number.

I have also discovered that when people do not know the exact number they may use the number *three*. They are not necessarily being deceptive. Instead, they are uncertain of what number to use so they automatically use the number *three*.

For twenty years, Al Michaels did play-by-play calling for *Monday Night Football* (MNF) which aired on the ABC network. In 2006, MNF moved from ABC to the ESPN cable network. Michaels along with his partner John Madden then switched to the NBC network to broadcast football on Sunday nights. In November 2005, Michaels was interviewed on HBO's *Real Sports with Bryant Gumbel*. In talking about leaving MNF, Michaels told Gumbell, "I've been doing Monday Night Football for twenty years. It feels like it's been about three."[18] Michaels could have said that it feels like it has been ten years which was half the time he spent at MNF. He could have chosen five years which is one fourth of the time. However, since he does not know exactly how many years it feels like, *three* is the number he chose to use.

On August 16, 2006, John Mark Karr was taken into custody in Bangkok, Thailand to face child pornography charges in the United States. Karr was also wanted for questioning in the murder of JonBenet Ramsey. On August 20, 2006, Karr was brought from Thailand to Los Angeles, California where he waited for an extradition hearing to Boulder, Colorado, the location where JonBenet was murdered. News crews gathered around the Boulder County Justice Center waiting for Karr's arrival in Boulder for his first court appearance which had yet to be scheduled. Boulder County court spokeswoman Karen Salaz stated that Karr would be advised of his rights during his first appearance. She further stated, "It's going to be three minutes max."[19] Salaz knows a first appearance hearing is generally a short hearing. However, there are various factors that can lengthen or shorten the hearing. She probably does not know exactly how long the hearing will last. Therefore, without realizing it she uses the number *three* in describing the length of the hearing.

During my career as a Deputy U.S. Marshal I spent many hours in the courtroom. When a judge decides to take a break he or she will state that court will be in recess. Typically, judges will declare the recess will be for ten or fifteen minutes. I remember one hearing in which a judge was deciding whether the defendant should be released on bond. Normally after both parties present their arguments for release or detention the judge immediately declares his decision. In this hearing, the prosecutor and the defense attorney both gave compelling arguments. I could sense the judge was uncertain of what he should do. After both attorneys finished speaking, the judge declared, "The court will take a three-minute recess." This was the only time in my twenty-six-year career that I heard a judge declare a three-minute recess. The reason the judge chose three minutes is because he was uncertain how long it would take him to make his decision. If he would have said five, ten, or fifteen minutes he probably would have come back into the courtroom close to those time periods. Out of curiosity, I timed the judge and he came back on the bench twelve minutes later. That was quadruple the amount of time he had said the recess would last.

If you want to detect deception, you should listen for the number *three*. This applies to time references, amounts of money, or numbers in general. When this number is used, explore that area within the statement to see if the person is giving you accurate information. One use of the number *three* does not automatically mean the person is lying. It may be that he did leave his house at 3:30 or he was robbed of $300. Also, remember that a person may be telling the truth but he does not know the exact number. This may cause him to use the number *three* as an estimate. Therefore, do not always accept the number *three* as the Gospel truth.

CHAPTER 3

Extra Words

One of the rules in Statement Analysis is that the shortest sentence is the best sentence. As an interviewer you want to obtain a lengthy statement. The more a person talks the more information you have to analyze. The more a person speaks the better the chance he will slip up if he is being deceptive. However, within a statement the short sentence is the best sentence. Prolonged sentences usually contain extra words. These extra words will provide you with extra information. To identify unnecessary words, see if there are words that can be taken out of the sentence and not change the essential meaning of the sentence. Many times these additional words will be qualifying words that alter the meaning of the statement.

On January 6, 1994, figure skater Nancy Kerrigan was preparing for the U.S. National Figure Skating Championship in Detroit, Michigan. After finishing her practice session, an unidentified assailant struck Kerrigan above the right knee with a metal police baton. The attacker got away and Kerrigan's injury kept her from competing in the competition.

Days after the attack the police identified Shane Stant as the hit man. An investigation discovered that Stant had been hired by two individuals, Shawn Eckardt and Jeff Gillooly, to carry out the attack. Eckardt was the bodyguard for skater Tonya Harding and Gillooly was Harding's ex-husband. The plan was to prevent Kerrigan from competing which would help Harding win the national championship. They were also hoping to make the other skaters fear for their safety. The conspirators planned to profit by being hired as bodyguards for the fearful skaters. Everyone speculated whether or not Tonya Harding had anything to do with the attack.

On January 11, 1994, Tonya Harding spoke to the media in regards to the incident. Her statement included the following denial: "I don't know for sure anything about what's going on at all."[1] We can shorten this sentence and still have it keep its meaning by saying, "I don't know anything about what's going on." Any other words used by Harding are extra words that are not needed as far as we, the reader, are concerned. However, Harding needs to put them into her statement. These extra words consist of *for sure* and *at all*. The reason Harding used the words *for sure* is because she is qualifying her statement. She wants us to believe that she does not know anything about what happened. However, that would be a lie. To avoid lying, she added the words *for sure*. What Harding is saying is that she does know something about this incident. She just does not know "for sure" all the details. A couple of weeks later we found out what Harding was hiding. On January 27, 1994, she admitted "I am responsible, however, for failing to report things I learned about the assault when I returned home from Nationals."[2]

The other extra words Harding used were *at all* which she placed at the end of the sentence; "I don't know for sure anything about what's going on at all." She does this in an attempt to convince us that she does not know anything about the incident. Deceptive people will often try and convince you they are telling the truth. This over emphasis is a sign she is being deceptive.

Paul Patton served as the governor of Kentucky from 1995 to 2003. In 2002, news surfaced that the governor had an extramarital affair with Tina Conner who operated a nursing home in Clinton, Kentucky. According to Connor, when she ended the affair, Patton turned state regulators onto her business which cited her for numerous health and safety violations. When the state pulled its Medicare and Medicaid funding from her facility she declared bankruptcy.

Governor Patton denied the affair and any retaliation against Connor or her business. In one statement he said, "In time, I expect that the full truth will come out. I think my conduct has been appropriate."[3] The governor gives a truthful statement in that the full truth will come out. It usually does. The last part of his statement is weak when he states, "I think my conduct has been appropriate." The word *think* tells us he is not certain if his conduct has been appropriate. A stronger statement would have been for him to not use the word *think* and simply say, "My conduct has been appropriate." Shortly after giving this statement the governor admitted to having the affair. He continues to deny he turned state regulators onto Connor's business.

The late Ted Kennedy was a United States Senator from Massachusetts. He had been in office since November 1962 until his death in August 2009. Earlier in his career on July 18, 1969,

Ted Kennedy attended a party on Chappaquiddick Island, Massachusetts. The party was a reunion for former aides to Robert Kennedy's 1968 presidential campaign. At around 11:00 p.m., Kennedy left the party and offered fellow party guest Mary Jo Kopechne a ride to her hotel. As Kennedy was attempting to leave the island he made a wrong turn and drove his Oldsmobile onto an unlit bridge that had no guard rails. He drove his car off the bridge and into Poucha Pond. The car overturned and came to rest upside down underwater. Kennedy was able to escape and swim to shore but Kopechne was not able to exit the vehicle and drowned. Instead of notifying the police, Kennedy went back to his hotel, called his attorney and went to bed. The next morning Kennedy called the police but the accident had already been discovered. In explaining his actions, Kennedy stated, "When I fully realized what happened this morning, I immediately contacted the police."[4] We can shorten his sentence to say, "When I realized what happened, I called the police." Kennedy wanted to downplay how much he remembered that night. However, the word *fully* tells us that Kennedy did realize something had happened. Once he had time to realize the magnitude of the situation, he then called the police. The words *this morning* and *immediately* are not needed but do add to the statement clarifying when these events occurred.

On February 24, 1994, Roger Altman, the Deputy Treasury Secretary in President Clinton's administration, testified before Congress. The Senate Banking Committee was looking into Bill and Hillary Clinton's real estate holdings which would become known as the Whitewater scandal. The senators were not pleased with Altman's testimony. Many of them felt he was withholding information on discussions the Treasury Department had with the White House concerning the ongoing investigations. In August of that year, the committee subpoenaed Joshua Steiner who was the Chief of Staff of the Treasury Department. Steiner's diary indicated that Altman may have discussed with President Clinton the Whitewater investigation. This seemed to contradict Altman's testimony and the White House's explanation on its role in the controversy.

In one line of questioning by Senator Paul Sarbanes from Maryland, the senator asked Steiner about the conversations he had with Altman and Jean Hanson the Treasury Department's general counsel. Unfortunately for Steiner, Senator Sarbanes is a very good listener.

Steiner: "I don't believe I had any specific conversations with either Mr. Altman or Ms. Hanson."
Sarbanes: "Strike the word specific."
Steiner: "I cannot recall any conversations where Mr. Altman said to me or Ms. Hanson said to me, 'I have a directly different recollection.'"
Sarbanes: "Strike the word directly."[5]

The senator recognizes that Steiner is qualifying his statement by adding the extra words *specific* and *directly*. This would eventually lead Steiner to make the following confession.

Steiner: "Senator, I have heard conversations where Mr. Altman has commented that his recollection is different from Ms. Hanson's."
Sarbanes: "You have heard such conversations?"
Steiner: "Yes."[6]

Earlier in his testimony Steiner said he could not recall any conversations where Altman or Hanson stated they had a "directly" different recollection. Now he starts to change his tune when he says, "I have heard conversations where Mr. Altman has commented that his recollection is different from Ms. Hanson's." This was brought to light because Senator Sarbanes recognized what Steiner was saying. In an effort to save Altman's job, Steiner was telling the truth. He never heard Altman mention that he had a "directly" different recollection of what occurred. However, he did hear Altman state he had a different, but not directly different, recollection. Senator Sarbanes concluded his questioning with the following comment.

> Sarbanes: "It's interesting because Mr. Altman did same the thing when he was before our committee and we have to parse your words very carefully."[7]

If you want to detect deception, look for any lengthy sentences within the statement. See if you can shorten the sentence by removing some of the words used by the subject. These extra words will provide you with extra information. Many times these additional words will be qualifying words that will change the meaning of the statement.

CHAPTER 4

Unusual Words and Phrases

Everything a person says has a meaning. There is a reason why a person will choose to put certain information into his story. There is also a reason why a person will phrase his statement in a certain way. In some cases, a statement may contain some unusual words or phrases. These odd statements should be obvious to see because of their strange wording.

On Friday evening, February 1, 2002, seven-year-old Danielle Van Dam disappeared from her home in a San Diego, California suburb. She was taken that night from her bedroom while she was sleeping. Her parents, Damon and Brenda Van Dam, called the police the next morning upon discovering their daughter was missing. As the police interviewed the neighbors they discovered that David Westerfield, who lived two doors away from the Van Dams, was not home. When Westerfield returned to his residence on Monday morning he was interviewed by the police. He told them he had spent the weekend alone driving around in his RV. He said that he went to the beach, the desert, and a campground. The police found it suspicious that Westerfield cleaned his RV when he returned home from his trip. He soon became a prime suspect in Danielle's disappearance and his RV was impounded. On February 22, 2002, Westerfield was arrested for kidnapping Danielle Van Dam after her blood was found in his RV. On February 27, 2002, volunteers found her decomposed body in a rural area east of San Diego.

During his police interview on February 4, 2002, Westerfield described driving around the countryside in his RV. In talking about a certain location he had visited, he was asked if he stopped and slept there. Westerfield replied with the following statement.

> "Well no. I stopped and ate and stuff like that and took a shower. I was pretty wasted. You know, working on the almost had a heart attack I think."[1]

The last sentence of his answer is a fragmented sentence. "You know, working on the almost had a heart attack I think." Earlier in the interview Westerfield told the detectives that during his excursion his RV became stuck in a rut. After about an hour of placing lawn chairs and other items under the tires to gain some traction, he was able to free his vehicle. In his fragmented sentence, Westerfield is referring back to this time when he was working on freeing his RV. The question is why did he stumble in his language? He is probably thinking about something else that was going on that he is not going to tell the detectives. This caused him to give a disjointed statement. We see further proof he was withholding information in his next answer where he describes what he did next.

> "Sat around for a little bit. And then decided to go on, go ahead and take off. This was the little place that we were, we were at was just a small turn-off type place."[2]

Westerfield told the detectives he alone during that weekend. However, he now uses the pronoun *we* which indicates someone was with him. (I will talk more about pronouns in the next chapter.) Westerfield was trying to hide the fact that Danielle was with him in his RV but his language betrayed him. It looks as if Westerfield may have realized what he had said since he stumbled on his words and repeated the phrase *we were*. This is also another indication he is thinking about what he should and should not say.

Despite his verbal slip-ups, Westerfield pled not guilty and went to trial on June 4, 2002. The prosecution presented evidence such as an orange fiber found on Danielle's body that was abundant in Westerfield's home. Blood stains found in the RV matched Danielle's DNA. On August 21, 2002, a jury found Westerfield guilty of kidnapping and murdering Danielle Van Dam. In January of 2003, he was sentenced to death for her slaying.

There was a man who said that his wife committed suicide by shooting herself in the head with a pistol. In his written statement to the police, the husband said that he and his wife were in their bedroom "playing around kind of half making out and stuff." The two of them then sat down on a waterbed. The husband then writes:

> "She got up off the waterbed and picked the pistol up from her dressing. I think but am not sure. She played with the gun a little and then put it to her temple because she knew people playing with knives or guns made me nervous. She smiled at me and said, 'You don't think I'll do it do you?' I smiled back

and told her no I didn't trying to hide my nervousness because I knew that was why she was teasing me in that way. The gun went off. I sat on the bed for about 5 to 10 seconds. I got up and went to where she fell."

The unusual statement can be found in the first sentence, "She got up off the waterbed and picked the pistol up from her dressing." Instead of saying his wife picked the pistol up from her dresser he wrote the word *dressing*. We know he is not illiterate because later in his story he writes that after his wife shot herself he picked the gun up and "threw it over by her dresser." He knows how to spell the word *dresser* so why did he write the word *dressing*?

As the police conducted their investigation they discovered this couple had martial problems. On the night she died, the husband was trying to make it sound like the two of them were fooling around. In reality, she was getting ready to leave him. In preparing to walk out of the house, what do you think she was doing? She was getting dressed. She was packing her suitcase. As the husband tells his lie the information that he does not want to share, the fact she was dressing, influences how he phrases his statement. Without realizing it he wrote the word *dressing* and not *dresser*. When confronted with other information found at the crime scene the husband admitted that he picked up the pistol and shot his wife.

Even without the unusual statement we can still see deception in the husband story. Let's say that he did use the word *dresser* and not *dressing*. His statement would then read, "She got up off the waterbed and picked the pistol up from her dresser." That sounds fine until we look at the next sentence where he writes, "I think but am not sure." As soon as he lies about his wife picking up the pistol he then qualifies his statement. What he is saying is, "I think that is what happened." "I am not sure if that is what happened." There were only two people in the house that night. One of them is dead and the other one is not sure what happened. We will revisit this statement later for more signs of deception.

In chapter two, I told the story of the husband who let his car roll off a cliff with his wife in the vehicle. We saw signs of deception in the first sentence of his statement when he used the unique word *with* in talking about his wife. At the end of his statement, he wrote the following two sentences.

"This is a tragic accident that how or why it happened. I never wanted to let her go and don't how this happened"

Both of these sentences have missing words which make the sentences fragmented. The husband probably wanted to write the sentences in the following manner.

"This is a tragic accident that *I don't know* how or why it happened. I never wanted to let her go and *I* don't *know* how this happened."

The problem is he did not write that. He wanted to tell the investigators that he did not know how this accident happened but he could not bring himself to write such a lie. As he is writing his deceptive story he is thinking about the truth and it causes him to stumble in his language and leave out some words.

On May 26, 2005, the senior class from Mountain Brook High School in Mountain Brook, Alabama went on an unofficial graduation trip to Aruba. One of the graduates on the trip was eighteen-year-old Natalee Holloway. On May 30, 2005, the last day of their trip, Holloway failed to appear for her flight home. Classmates stated she was last seen on May 30 around 1:30 a.m. outside an Aruban night club called Carlos'n Charlie's. Natalee was with Dutch national Joran van der Sloot and two of his friends Deepak and Satish Kalpoe. The three young men initially told investigators they dropped Natalee off at her hotel. After further questioning, they changed their story and said they dropped her and Van der Sloot off at the beach near the Marriott Hotel at about 1:40 a.m. Van der Sloot claims that around 3:00 a.m. Satish Kalpoe picked him up and they left Natalee alone on the beach. She has not been seen since.

On June 9, 2005 Van der Sloot and the Kalpoe brothers were arrested for reasonable suspicion of murder and manslaughter involving Natalee's disappearance. They were denied bond and taken into custody. Lacking hard evidence that a murder had occurred, on September 3, 2005 the three suspects were released from police custody. Natalee remains missing and the case remains open with Van der Sloot as the chief suspect in her disappearance.

On March 1, 2006, the FOX News show On *The Record w/Greta Van Susteren* aired part one of Greta Van Susteren's interview with Joran van der Sloot. Van der Sloot described being in the bar Carlos'n Charlie's with Natalee on the night of May 30. He stated they left the bar around 1:00 a.m. and were walking to the car hand-in-hand. Satish Kalpoe was with them and Deepak Kalpoe was waiting in the car. We then have the following question and answer.

Van Susteren:	"Any discussion between Carlos'n Charlie's and the car between you and Satish or you and Natalee?"
Van der Sloot:	"No, just between me and Natalee. We were speaking English to each other and I asked her if she wanted to go back to her hotel and that's when she said that she wanted to."[3]

Van Susteren asked him if any discussion took place while they were walking to the car. She suggests that perhaps Van der Sloot and Satish Kalpoe had a conversation. Van der Sloot says the only discussion was "just between me and Natalee." He then mentions something unusual; "We were speaking English to each other." Why does Van der Sloot state they were speaking "English" to each other? He never mentions this at any other time during his interview. What this tells us is that somebody, at some point, was not speaking English. When the conversation switched back to English this led Van der Sloot to unknowingly include this in his statement. I believe Van der Sloot speaks Dutch. Perhaps Natalee picked up a little Dutch while in Aruba and was trying to converse with Van der Sloot in Dutch. Maybe he was teaching her the Dutch language. When their conversation in Dutch was not going well, they decided to start "speaking English to each other." That's one possible reason. A more sinister explanation is that the three boys, Van der Sloot and the Kalpoe brothers were speaking to each other in Dutch so Natalee would not know what they were saying. Perhaps they were discussing their plans for the night. When Van der Sloot stopped talking to the Kalpoe brothers in Dutch and turned his attention to Natalee, this caused him to say, "We were speaking English to each other."

It would take two years before we found out why Joran van der Sloot used the word "English" in his interview with Greta Van Susteren. In 2007, Dutch businessman Patrick van der Eem befriended Van der Sloot. After gaining his trust, Van der Eem went to Holland's leading investigative reporter Peter R. de Vries and set up a six month sting operation to record Van der Eem's conversations with Van der Sloot. The secretly taped recordings were made in a Range Rover that was driven by Van der Eem with Van der Sloot sitting in the passenger seat. Van der Eem played the role of a gangster and asked Van der Sloot if he was interested in starting a marijuana operation. Van der Sloot said he was interested in getting into the business. As the months went by Van der Eem and Van der Sloot began to develop a friendship. Van der Eem used this opportunity to get Van der Sloot to open up about what happened to Natalee Holloway.

In February 2008, the ABC News program *20/20* aired portions of Van der Sloot's taped conversations with Van der Eem. In describing leaving the nightclub Carlos'n Charlie's on the night Natalee disappeared, Van der Sloot made the following statement.

> "So I was with her and I said to the guys, 'I want to go somewhere alone with her but she doesn't want to go to her hotel.' I also kind of want to do what she wants, that's how it is you know. I say, 'Just drop us off at the beach. Then I'll fuck her and take her to the hotel after.' So they dropped me off at the beach. I get out and walk with her to the beach. I'm kissing her and stuff but she doesn't look so hot, you know.

She was looking kind of pale too. But she wanted it. She really wanted it."[4]

Van der Sloot states that while he was in the car with Natalee and the Kalpoe brothers, he told the Kalpoe brothers "Just drop us off at the beach. Then I'll fuck her and take her to the hotel after." That is a pretty bold and rude statement to make in the presence of a young lady. However, if Van der Sloot made that statement in Dutch, then Natalee would not have known what he had said. After telling the brothers of his plans for the night, he then starts talking to Natalee in English.

Van der Sloot went on to tell Van der Eem that while he and Natalee were on the beach she went into convulsions and passed out. Thinking that she was dead Van der Sloot called a friend who took Holloway out to sea and disposed of her body in the ocean. After this story broke, Van der Sloot would state that he made up this story in order to fit in with Van der Eem the alleged gangster. Despite his denials we have a statement made by Van der Sloot in 2006 that ties in with a statement he made a couple of years earlier. Over the years, other suspects in Natalee's disappearance have been questioned but no charges have been filed. Natalee Holloway's vanishing remains a mystery.

On a summer evening in August 2002, Justin Barber and his wife April took a stroll along the beach in St. Augustine, Florida. They had just finished dinner and were celebrating their third wedding anniversary. Their romantic walk ended when a man carrying a gun approached them on the beach. According to Justin Barber the agitated man wanted money. When the man pointed the gun at the couple Justin Barber stepped in between the man and April. A shot rang out and Justin struggled with the man to gain control of the gun. Justin then said he passed out and when he awoke he could not find his wife. He ran up and down the beach looking for April only to find her floating face down in the surf. It appeared she had been shot. He attempted to drag her off the beach to get her help but he had to give up because of the gunshot wounds he had received. He left April near a walkway and went to the coastal highway in an attempt to wave down a motorist. He was unable to get any cars to stop so he got into his vehicle. Someone saw that Justin was in distress and called 911. The police found him slumped behind the wheel of his car. When the evening was over, April Barber was dead with a gunshot wound to the face. Justin Barber survived with several superficial gunshot wounds.

In a written statement to the police, Justin Barber described what occurred on the beach. As he and April were walking along the edge of the water Barber looked up and saw a man in front of them about ten feet away. Barber then writes, "As he approached, the yelled something at me."[5] Barber clearly wrote the word *the* when probably meant to write the word *he* as in "he yelled something at me." Writing the wrong word indicates that Barber was thinking about something else and did not realize what he had written. Perhaps he was thinking about what actually occurred which caused him to stumble in his language. We will revisit this case in chapter eleven.

If you want to detect deception and obtain additional information, look for fragmented or unusual phrases within a story. These types of statements should jump out at you because of the way they are worded. Ask yourself why did he say it that way or why did he include this in his story? Sometimes this will be the most important information in the statement. Therefore, it is worth looking into and trying to determine exactly what was going on at this point in the story.

CHAPTER 5

Pronouns

You can learn a lot by listening to the pronouns used by an individual. We all know that plural pronouns such as *we, us,* and *they* indicate more than one person was present. Some people would argue the pronoun *they* (or its inflected forms) can be used as a "singular they." In this world of political correctness, some people feel we should not use a masculine pronoun in a gender neutral sentence. For example, some people believe the statement, "If anyone is sick, he should go to his doctor" is politically incorrect because the pronoun *anyone* can refer to either sex. Constantly using "he or she" or the hybrid "s/he" to avoid the sexist overtones seems awkward in speech and in writing. Therefore, some people resort to using the "singular they" to keep the sentence neutral; "If anyone is sick, they should go to their doctor."

I don't have a problem using the "singular they" because in my opinion it is never truly singular. If a teacher is addressing a class of twenty students, some people believe that it would be correct for the teacher to say, "If anyone is sick, they should go see the doctor." However, if only one pupil was sitting in the classroom, it would be very odd for the teacher to say, "If anyone is sick, they should go see the doctor." Since the teacher is addressing one student, a better statement would be, "If you are sick, you should go see the doctor." Even though the word *anyone* is considered a singular pronoun, it is only used when there is more than one person present. Maybe only one person went to the doctor but there were others who could have gone. Because words such as *anyone, everyone, anybody,* and *everybody* can refer to more than one person, it is acceptable to use the plural pronoun *they*. If the antecedent is without a doubt singular, then you cannot use the "singular they." In my opinion, every time you see the pronoun *they* it means plurality; there was more than one person present. The term "singular they" could be better described as the "generic they."

There is no argument that the pronouns *we* and *us* always indicate plurality. What you may not realize is that these pronouns also indicate there is a partnership between the participants. We may not know how much of a partnership exists but these pronouns do show us there is a relationship. Therefore, we would not expect to find the pronouns *we* or *us* in a kidnapping or rape statement. The victim is not going to partner up with the attacker. Consider the following statement given by a rape victim.

> "He forced me into his car and drove me to an abandoned house. We went into the house and he raped me."

At a glance, the statement sounds believable until we look at the pronouns and discover the subject used the pronoun *we*. By saying, "We went into the house" the subject is telling us she was a willing participant. Her language gives the impression that the two of them were affably walking into the house together. If this were a truthful statement, the victim would probably state that she was dragged or forced into the house. I have seen cases where the sex was consensual. When the woman's boyfriend found out she had sex with another man she then claimed it was rape. However, the pronoun *we* in her statement showed she was a willing participant. The other possible reason why the pronoun *we* will show up in a sexual assault statement is because the person is making up the story. Because she was not raped, it is hard for her to tell the story from the perspective of being attacked. This causes her to unknowingly use the pronoun *we*.

Pronouns give us responsibility. Sometimes people do not want to take responsibility for their actions. Therefore, they will use pronouns such as *we* and *us* to spread the blame. Instead of saying, "I should have done a better job" they will say, "We should have done a better job" even though it was their responsibility to get the job done. There was a federal judge who was presiding over a case involving General Electric. Several days into the trial it was discovered the judge owned stock in General Electric. The judge then did the right thing and dismissed himself from the case. He then released the following statement.

> "I really thought we had a system in place to eliminate situations like this. You know, you try to avoid these problems, but apparently in this case we did not. In the future, we will ensure that I excuse myself from other cases involving General Electric."

The judge starts off using the pronoun *I* but then shifts to the pronoun *you*. "You try to avoid these problems." He did not say, "I try to avoid these problems." He was pointing his finger back at you and me. He then goes on to say that in this case "we did not" avoid these problems. He could have said "I did not" but he does not want to take full responsibility for his actions. He wants to blame his secretary, law clerks and anyone else that works with him so he uses the pronoun *we*.

We all get those sweepstake notifications in the mail telling us that we have won a large sum of money. Most people are skeptical that good fortune has come their way. To verify their suspicion, they read the fine print. However, you can tell what is going on without reading the fine print. The last winner's notification I received started out with the following statement.

> "I am pleased to inform you that you are to receive a cash amount. We are currently holding a corporate check in the amount of $5,000 and await the filing of your Winning's Claim form."

Pronouns show possession. The first sentence clearly states that I (you) will receive a cash amount. Great, I can always use a few extra bucks. So, how much money am I going to win? The second sentence mentions $5,000 but look at the pronouns in this sentence; "We are currently holding a corporate check in the amount $5,000..." (I believe they have a check in amount of $5,000.) "...and await the filing of your Winning Claims form." (I believe they are waiting for me to return my Winning Claims form.) No where does it state that the $5,000 is mine. What is missing is the pronoun *you*. They didn't say, "We are currently holding a corporate check in the amount of $5,000 for you" or "We are currently holding your check worth $5,000." By stating in the first sentence that I have won some money, they are hoping I will believe the $5,000 mentioned in the second sentence is mine. Out of curiosity I read the fine print. Odds are I am going to win $1.00!

You can sometimes detect admissions by looking at the pronouns in a statement. This is possible because pronouns give us responsibility and people will sometimes unknowingly take responsibility for the act. We see this in the Steven Truscott case. In 1959, 14-year-old Steven Truscott was convicted in a Canadian courtroom of raping and murdering 12-year-old classmate Lynne Harper. Lynne was last seen with Truscott as the two of them rode across the school yard on his bicycle. Truscott claims he dropped Lynne off at an intersection where she was going to walk to a house that had some ponies. As he peddled his bike back towards the school he said he saw a car stop along the road and he saw Lynne get into the car. The next day Lynne Harper's body was found not far from where Truscott dropped her off.

After serving ten years in prison, Truscott was paroled and wrote a book about his ordeal entitled *The Steven Truscott Story*. The book was co-authored by Bill Trent. In his book, Truscott talks about the press and how one reporter referred to him as being "clever and devious."[1] Truscott took exception to this comment and writes the following in his book.

> "As to 'clever and devious' had I intended to rape and murder Lynne Harper would I not rather have been stupid beyond belief to drive my victim minutes prior to killing her past innumerable witnesses? This fact occurred to no one not even my counsel."[2]

In talking about the victim Lynne Harper, Truscott does not state that he drove *her* past innumerable witnesses. He does not state that he drove *the victim* past these witnesses. What he tells us is that he drove "my victim." By using the pronoun *my*, Truscott was taking possession of the victim. He was telling us that he killed Lynne Harper. Truscott mentioned "my counsel" which was his counsel. When he wrote "my victim" Lynne Harper became his victim. If co-author Bill Trent was responsible for this language, we would expect him to refer to Lynne Harper as "her" or "the victim." If Bill Trent wrote "my victim" it tells us he believes Truscott was responsible for Lynne's death.

We see further evidence in his book that Truscott was involved in Lynne Harper's murder when we analyze his language. After being found guilty, Truscott was sentenced to death. He became the youngest person to sit on Canada's death row. Fortunately for Truscott, he received a stay of execution. He talks about his stay of execution in his book.

> "This was the first news I received that a stay of execution had been ordered. I often wonder when I would have been told, had it not been for that guard. I was dazed and it was some time before the full significance of what had occurred got through to me. I wasn't going to die! Hastily, I qualified my jubilance. I wasn't going to die as soon as I'd expected. But Pop used to say, 'Where there's life there's hope' and I was alive! Perhaps there would be yet another miracle, an appeal, a new trial, even an acquittal."[3]

One of the things you want to look for in a statement is what hasn't the person told you. After receiving his stay of execution, Truscott hopes for another miracle. He then lists three things he would like to see happen; "an appeal, a new trial, even an acquittal." A successful "appeal" may overturn his conviction and give Truscott a "new trial." He is then hopeful a new trial would win him his freedom which would be "an acquittal." However, what is Truscott not telling us? If you were an innocent person sitting on death row, what would be the greatest miracle of all that would give you your freedom? It would of course be that the person who killed Lynne Harper was caught and confessed to the murder. Not only would you be set free but you would be completely exonerated. That is much better than receiving a new trial and being acquitted. Yet Truscott never asks for that. It never crosses his mind that the best thing for him would be for the killer to be found. To him, this isn't an option because he knows he killed Lynne Harper.

On August 28, 2007, the Ontario Court of Appeals acquitted Steven Truscott of the 1959 killing of Lynne Harper. What the court did not do was declare him innocent of this crime. His defense team had asked the court for a declaration of innocence. The court ruled "the appellant (Truscott) has not demonstrated his factual innocence." They went on to say, "We are in no position to make a declaration of innocence. Indeed we are not satisfied that an acquittal would be the only reasonable verdict."[4] Normally, the case would be retried but the court also ruled that with the passing of time some witnesses and evidence were no longer available making it difficult to have a second trial.

On June 17, 1994, O.J. Simpson was to be arrested via voluntary surrender for the murder of his ex-wife Nicole Brown Simpson and her friend Ronald Goldman. Instead of surrendering, Simpson and his friend, Al Cowlings, got into Cowling's Ford Bronco and according to Simpson headed for the cemetery to visit Nicole's grave. Because of a police presence at the cemetery Simpson was unable to visit her grave site. Simpson then claims Cowlings noticed that Simpson had a gun. Fearing Simpson might shoot himself Cowlings called the police on his cell phone and told them he had Simpson and he was taking him back to his house. What followed was the infamous slow speed Bronco chase which was televised to millions of viewers. During the chase detective Tom Lange spoke with Simpson on a cell phone. Simpson was huddled in the back seat of the Bronco with a gun in his hand. Lange spends the entire conversation trying to convince Simpson to throw away the gun. At this point in time, Simpson is suicidal. Here are some excerpts from this taped conversation.

Simpson: "I just need to get to my house. I can't live with (unintelligible)."

Lange: "We're going to do that. Just throw the gun out the window."

Simpson: "I can't do that."

Lange: "We're not going to bother you. We're going to let you go up there. Just throw it out the window. Please. You're scaring everybody. O.J., you there?"

Simpson: "— for me. This is not to keep you guys away from me. This is for me."

Lange: "Okay. It's for you, I know that. But do it for —"
Simpson: "This is for me, for me. That's all."[5]

There is no doubt Simpson is contemplating suicide. He tells us the gun is not to keep the police away but it is for him. We see further evidence of his suicidal state when later in the conversation he makes the statements, "Ah, just tell them I'm all sorry."[6] "I've said goodbye to my kids."[7] What follows is Simpson's confession that he murdered Nicole Brown Simpson.

Lange: "Don't do this. They love you. Don't do it, O.J. It's going to work itself out. It's going to work. It's going to work. You're listening to me, I know you are, and you're thinking about your kids right now, aren't you? Aren't you?"
Simpson: "Ah –"
Lange: "They're thinking about you. They're thinking about you."
Simpson: "Ah –"
Lange: "So is your mother. Your mother loves you. Everybody loves you. Don't do this."
Simpson: "Oh –"
Lange: "I know you're thinking."
Simpson: "Oh –"
Lange: "Man, just throw it out the window."
Simpson: "Ah –"
Lange: "And nobody's going to get hurt."
Simpson: "I'm the only one that deserves it."
Lange: "No, you don't deserve that."
Simpson: "I'm going to get hurt."

Lange:	"You do not deserve to get hurt."
Simpson:	"Ah –"
Lange:	"Don't do this."
Simpson:	"All I did was love Nicole. That's all I did was love her."
Lange:	"I understand."[8]

Did you see the confession? It occurs right after Lang tells Simpson, "nobody's going to get hurt." Simpson responds by saying, "I'm the only one that deserves it." The murder of his ex-wife has placed Simpson in this suicidal state. It is in this setting he tells us through his use of the pronoun *I* that he is the only one who deserves to die. If these murders were committed by someone else, wouldn't that person be worthy of death?

The slow speed Bronco chase ended at Simpson's residence where he was taken into custody and charged with two counts of murder. He was jailed and denied bail. In an effort to raise money for his defense, Simpson wrote a book entitled, *I Want To Tell You*. The book contains letters that people had written to Simpson while he was in jail and Simpson's response to those letters. Most of the letters were pro Simpson. However, Simpson did publish some letters in which the writers felt that Simpson was responsible for these murders. On page thirteen of his book, Simpson thanks these people for allowing him to publish their letters.

> "I am grateful that even those who believe in my guilt also believe that I should have my day in court and have agreed to let their words be published in this book."[9]

Simpson takes responsibility for these murders when he uses the phrase "my guilt." The pronoun *my* is a possessive pronoun. Simpson is saying there are people who believe in something that he has already established – "my guilt." Notice he did not say, "I am grateful that even those who believe I am guilty." In this statement, the writer is not admitting he is guilty. He is only saying there are people who believe he is guilty. That is probably how you would phrase this statement since you are an innocent party. Simpson however, chose to phrase his statement based on his guilt. In this same statement, Simpson talks about having "my day in court." That was his day in court and that was also his guilt.

In the middle 1970s, mysterious crop circles began to appear in Southern England. These designs were usually in a circular formation impressed upon fields of wheat, oats or barley. The phenomenon progressed year by year moving across the ocean to the United States. By the late 1980s and early 1990s, country sides were adorned with geometrical figures imprinted on fields of grain. Many people believed these formations were created by flying saucers which had landed in the fields. The idea this was a hoax seemed impossible. There were hundreds of crop circles. They seemed to appear rather quickly and on such a large scale. There were no footprints leading to or going from the formations. Many people concluded they must be of an extraterrestrial origin.

In 1991, Doug Bower and Dave Chorley from Southampton, England, admitted they had been making the crop figures for 15 years. It was something they had dreamed up one night over a few drinks. They even demonstrated to the press how they performed their nocturnal artwork. The circles which appeared in other countries were apparently copycat hoaxers. It turns out we didn't have to wait 15 years to see this was a hoax. On one of their night time operations, Bower and Chorley decided to leave a message. In one of their circles, they left the letters WEARENOTALONE. A quick examination of the letters reveals the sentence "We are not alone." Some people thought this was a sign of intelligent life. However, the only sign this statement was giving is that this indeed was a practical joke. If aliens had landed on our planet and were going to leave us a message, it wouldn't say, "We are not alone." It would read, "You are not alone." The pronouns give it away.

In addition to revealing a confession, pronouns can also show if a person is tense and therefore possibly being deceptive. The key is to look for the pronoun *I* and how many times it is used. A person who is under some stress may overuse this pronoun. Consider the following statement which makes great use of the pronoun *I*.

> "I woke up at 7:00. I took a shower and I made breakfast. I read the newspaper and I checked my emails while I was eating breakfast. I left the house at 8:00 and I arrived at work at 8:25. I was at work until 5:00. I then drove home and I was in my house the rest of the evening."

In order to tell us what he did, the subject must use the pronoun *I*. However, there are several times in his statement where he could have omitted the use of the pronoun *I*. For example, he could have stated, "I took a shower and made breakfast." Because he began the sentence with the pronoun *I* it is understood that he is referring to himself when he mentions making breakfast. The word *and* connects the two actions of taking a shower and making breakfast. The same is true for checking his emails and arriving at work. The excessive use of the pronoun *I* indicates the subject is under some stress. He may be trying too hard to convince us that he did what he said he did.

The lack of the pronoun *I* in a statement is an indication the person is not committed to his story. If we are to believe a person did something, the person has to tell us he did it by using the pronoun *I*. If the pronoun *I* is missing, then we cannot believe the subject performed the action unless there is a justifiable reason why the *I* is missing. Look at the following statement that is missing the pronoun *I*.

> "Woke up and got dressed. Drank a cup of coffee and watched the news on TV. Left the house around 7:40. Arrived at work at 8:20. Worked until 5:30 and then drove home. Made dinner and watched the football game. Went to bed after the game was over."

The subject wants us to believe that he woke up, got dressed, drank a cup of coffee, etc. The problem is he does not tell us that he (I) did these things. There is no subject in this statement. We do not know who carried out these actions. We cannot believe he performed these tasks since he does not claim responsibility.

It could be that the subject did do all of these things but for some reason he does not want to tell us that he did them. Not using the pronoun *I* may be his way of telling us what he did without directly referring to himself. He may have done something else that he wants to keep hidden.

In April of 1993, President Clinton appeared in public with some scratches on his face. The press speculated that perhaps the First Lady threw something at the President or scratched him with her fingernails. The media inquired about the scratches but the President was mum about the subject. The White House press secretary Dee Dee Myers said, "I believe the president cut himself shaving."[10] Recognize the word "believe" means Myers does not know for certain the president cut himself shaving. Later that day during an Oval Office photo session, the President explained the cuts on his face.

> "I got this playing with my daughter I'm ashamed to say. Rolling around acting like a child again. I reaffirmed that I'm not a kid anymore."[11]

The first and last sentences begin with the pronoun *I*. However, the second sentence does not have a subject. President Clinton did not say, "I was rolling around acting like a child again." The reason the pronoun *I* is missing can be found in the first sentence; "I'm ashamed to say." The President was embarrassed by this incident. Therefore, when he decided to tell us in detail what happened he left himself out of the story.

When a person changes his pronouns this is an indication he is being deceptive. It should be quite obvious if a person uses the pronoun *he* in his statement and then later changes it to *she*. Unless the person he is talking about has the ability to transform into another sex we have a problem. Perhaps there were more people involved and he was trying his best not to reveal that information. However, his choice of pronouns betrayed him.

Detecting deception with changing pronouns is more often seen when a person shifts from a pronoun to an article such as from *my* to *the*. We see this in the following statement about a house that went up in flames. Look for the changing pronouns, and see if you can determine approximately what time the house was set on fire.

> "I left my house around 11:30 a.m. and met Jim Johnson for lunch at Applebee's. We left the restaurant around 1:00 p.m. and went to my house to watch a baseball game. The game was over at 4:00 p.m. Jim and I then decided to go to the movies to see The Green Hornet. Jim had to run a few errands so we agreed to meet at the movie theater at 7:15 p.m. Jim left my house shortly after 4:00 p.m. I watched a little more TV and ate a snack. At 7:00 p.m., I left the house and met Jim at the movies. The movie was over at 9:45 p.m. I then left the movie theater and headed home. Around 10:00 p.m. I saw fire trucks in my neighborhood and discovered that my house had caught on fire."

The subject begins his statement referring to his residence as "my house." The pronoun *my* is a possessive pronoun. He continues to call it "my house" up to 4:00 p.m. However, at 7:00 p.m. he said he left "the house" to meet Jim at the movies. At 7:00 p.m., he no longer took possession of his house because he used the article *the*. When he changed his language from *my* to *the* he was distancing himself from his house. The reason he no longer wanted to take possession of his house is because he knew it was on fire. Shortly before he left his house at 7:00 p.m. he set his house on fire.

On October 25, 1994, Susan Smith from Union, South Carolina reported to the police that a black male had stolen her car along with her two children who were in the backseat. The authorities were on the lookout for Smith's car, her two boys and a male suspect. Smith made tearful pleas for the man to release her children. In one of her pleas made on November 2, 1994, Smith gave the following statement.

> "I would like to say to whoever has my children that they please, I mean please bring 'em home to us where they belong."[12]

Smith first refers to the carjacker using the pronoun *whoever*. She is acting as if she has no idea who abducted her kids. However, she supposedly does know a little about the kidnapper because she was able to give a description of him. Not only does she know what he looks like but she may also know what he sounds like and maybe what he smells like. Even though she does not know the kidnapper's name she should still refer to him as "the man who has my children."

Secondly, she refers to the kidnapper as *they*. Here Smith changes her pronouns from a single carjacker to multiple carjackers. So where does the *they* come from? It comes from her deceptive mind. Because she is making up the story she cannot relate to it. She cannot see one man driving away with her kids because it never happened. Therefore, she slips up and uses the pronouns *whoever* and *they*. As soon as I saw her make this plea on television I knew she was lying. The following day Smith confessed that she killed her two boys by driving to John D. Long Lake, parking her car on the ramp, getting out of the car and letting her car drive into the lake with her two boys seat belted and trapped in the back seat.

We also see changing pronouns in Smith's confession. In describing being at the lake and contemplating suicide, Smith gave the following statement.

> "When I was @ John D. Long Lake, I had never felt so scared and unsure as I did then. I wanted to end my life so bad and was in my car ready to go down that ramp into the water, and I did go part way, but I stopped. I went again and stopped. I then got out of the car and stood by the car a nervous wreck."[13]

The change in pronouns occurs when she references her car. She first calls it "my car" and then calls it "the car." When Smith uses the phrase "my car" she is claiming possession of her car. When she refers to it as "the car" she is distancing herself from her car. If she was describing her car going into the water with her two boys in the backseat, we would expect her to say "the car." No one would want to take possession of that fateful car. However, she is allegedly standing outside of her car trying to decide what to do. Therefore, she should have referred to it as "my car." She should have said, "I then got out of my car and stood by my car a nervous wreck." By calling it "the car" she unknowingly tells us she knew what she was going to do. She could see "the car" going into the water with her out of "the car" and her two boys in "the car." There was no last minute jumping out of the car while the car rolled into the water. She purposely sent her car into the water to drown her two boys presumably because the man she loved did not want any kids. That is what the jury decided when they convicted her on two counts of murder.

It should be noted that the pronoun *my* not only shows possession but it also uniquely identifies the object. Once the object has been identified with the pronoun *my*, it is normal for people to then use the definite article *the*. The key to seeing if the person is being deceptive is to look at where the change occurs. For example, it would have been alright for Susan Smith to state, "I then got out of my car and stood by the car a nervous wreck." Once she uniquely identifies the car in that sentence with the pronoun *my*, she then uses the definite article. In the case in which the house burned down, we see the writer consistently used the pronoun *my* and only one time used the definite article *the* in regards to his house.

If you want to detect deception, listen to the pronouns used by the subject. Remember that the pronouns *we* and *us* always indicate there is a partnership. Look to see if it is appropriate that a partnership existed. Pronouns show responsibility. Some people do not want to take responsibility for their actions and will use plural pronouns to spread the blame. Other times people will unknowingly take responsibility for what happened by the pronouns they use. Look to see if the pronouns show a confession. Pay attention to the pronoun *I*. Overuse of this pronoun indicates the person is tense and may be lying. If the pronoun *I* is missing, you cannot believe the person did what he claimed to have done since there is no subject. Lastly, look to see if the person changed any pronouns and if the change is justifiable or a sign of deception.

CHAPTER 6

Verb Tenses

When we solicit information we are usually inquiring about something that happened in the past. If you are conducting a criminal investigation you are looking to gather facts about what happened at the crime scene. If you are interviewing a job applicant, you are gathering information about the person's experience and accomplishments. Since the interviewee is telling you what happened, he should be speaking in the past tense. When a person is making up a story he will sometimes use present tense language. This is because he is not telling his story from memory but he is creating it as he speaks to the interviewer. Since he is presently constructing his story, present tense language may enter into his statement. We see this in the following statement.

> "I was in my car stopped at a red light. A man approached my car and points a gun at me. He tells me to get out of the car."

If you give this statement a quick read, it may appear that everything sounds all right. However, when you look at the verb tenses you see the subject started out using past tense verbs (was, stopped, approached) but then shifted to present tense verbs (points, tells). If this were a truthful statement, the person should have said that a man approached his car and *pointed* a gun at him. The man then *told* him to get out of the car. It may be the subject started out using past tense language because nearly everyone at some point in time has been sitting in their car at a red light waiting for it to turn green. Most people can also relate to someone approaching their car and asking for directions, a donation, or to clean their windshield. Therefore, the subject can search his memory and talk about this in the past tense. When it comes time to tell a lie about being carjacked the subject has no memory of this incident to rely upon. Consequently, he unknowingly uses present tense language.

People will also use present tense language to avoid answering a question. Consider the following question and answer.

Question: "Have you ever smoked marijuana?"
Answer: "I don't smoke marijuana."

The subject was asked if in his entire lifetime he had ever smoked marijuana. He responded by saying that he presently does not smoke marijuana (I don't). He may have smoked a joint the day before but in his mind he is giving a truthful answer because five minutes ago he decided to quit! The subject did not address any past usage. A good answer that would cover his lifetime would be to say "No" or "I have never smoked marijuana." The use of the unique word *never* would be appropriate because he was asked if he had *ever* smoked marijuana. Remember, the word *never* means not ever.

President Clinton used present tense language to avoid answering a question. (I don't mean to pick on the former President but he sure gave us plenty of examples.) On January

21, 1998, the President was interviewed by Jim Lehrer on the PBS show *News Hour*. Lehrer began the interview by asking the President about his relationship with 24-year-old former White House intern Monica Lewinsky. The President denied he asked Ms. Lewinsky to lie under oath stating, "I did not ask anyone to tell anything other than the truth."[1] Lehrer then questions the President about his relationship with Ms. Lewinsky.

Lehrer: "You had no sexual relationship with this young woman?"

Clinton: "There is not a sexual relationship. That is accurate"[2]

The question could be better worded by asking, "Did you have a sexual relationship with this young woman?" The way Lehrer phrased the question he was basically stating that the President did not have a sexual relationship with Ms. Lewinsky. All Lehrer was doing was looking for the President to confirm this by saying, "I did not have a sexual relationship with her." However, the President did not say that. Instead he said, "There is not a sexual relationship." This is a truthful statement. At the time of the interview, the President was not having a relationship with Ms. Lewinsky. The problem is he was speaking in the present tense. He did not deny that there ever was a sexual relationship. On August 17, 1998, President Clinton addressed the nation and stated, "I did have a relationship with Miss Lewinsky that was not appropriate. In fact, it was wrong."[3] The President did not describe the relationship as being sexual in nature but most people believe it was.

Joey Buttafuoco played the tense game. In May 1992, someone walked up to the Buttafuoco residence in Massapequa, New York and knocked on the front door. When Buttafuoco's wife, Mary Jo, opened the door she was shot in the face. Fortunately, she survived the shooting. The investigation into her attempted murder led to the arrest of a 17-year-old named Amy Fisher whom the press would refer to as the Long Island Lolita. Fisher told the police she and Buttafuoco were having an affair and that he wanted her to kill his wife. Fisher pled guilty to shooting Mary Jo Buttafuoco and was sentenced to five to fifteen years in prison. Joey Buttafuoco pled guilty to statutory rape and was given a six month sentence.

At the onset of the investigation, Buttafuoco denied any sexual involvement with Fisher. In 1992, Buttafuoco told radio host Howard Stern, "Let me tell you something. I don't cheat on my wife. No. Oh no. Oh no."[4] However, in 1993 when Buttafuoco pled guilty to statutory rape, he stated that he had sexual relations with Amy Fisher at the Freeport Hotel in 1991. We know by his own court admission he had an affair with Fisher in 1991. So, how can Joey Buttafuoco in 1992 make a statement denying an affair? It is because in 1992 he was telling the truth. He didn't say, "I have never cheated on my wife." He didn't say, "I didn't cheat on my wife." What he said was, "I don't cheat on my wife." His reply was in the present tense. With all the publicity he was getting, he probably was not cheating on his wife in 1992. However, he did not tell us he never cheated on his wife. Buttafuoco only tried to deny he had an affair.

The Tour de France is the most prestigious bicycle race in the world. The race lasts three weeks and is broken down into segments called stages. A rider's time to finish each stage is recorded and the cyclist with the lowest aggregate time for all of the stages is declared the winner. In 2006, American cyclist Floyd Landis won the Tour de France. Despite losing ten minutes during Stage 16, Landis suspiciously came back strong during Stage 17. After completing Stage 17, Landis tested positive for banned synthetic testosterone. He was then stripped of his victory.

At a news conference held on July 28, 2006 in Madrid, Spain, Landis stated this was not a blood doping case but that he has a natural a high level of testosterone. Landis further stated, "I would like to make absolutely clear that I am not in any doping process."[5] Landis gives his denial in the present tense; "I am not in any doping process." In his mind, this is a truthful statement. At the time he was giving the news conference, he was not participating in the doping process. What is missing is Landis telling us that he has never engaged in blood doping or that he did not dope while participating in the 2006 Tour de France.

Despite losing his title Landis maintained his innocence for several years. Then in 2010, Landis told ESPN.com "I want to clear my conscience. I don't want to be part of the problem any more."[6] In emails sent to cycling officials and sponsors, Landis admitted he had been doping since 2002.

When I worked for the U.S. Marshals Service we had a case in which a man was convicted of federal income tax evasion. Despite facing a long prison sentence, the judge allowed the man to remain on bond prior to his sentencing. Several days before he was to be sentenced he disappeared while scuba diving with his son. His body was never found and the family presumed he had drowned.

Government prosecutors thought the father and his son had staged the accident so the father could avoid going to prison. It was believed the two men got the idea from one of their friends who had died in a scuba diving accident. After six months of searching, we had not found the father or his body. The government then put pressure on the son by making him testify at a deposition. Under oath he would have to state he did not know the whereabouts of his father. During the deposition the Assistant U.S. Attorney asked the son about the friend who had drowned in a similar accident.

> Question: "This was in much clearer water when this occured right?"
> Answer: "Yes."
> Question: "Your father knew that someone had died as a result of this accident?"
> Answer: "I don't know for definite that he knows. I would guess that he would probably know. I don't know for sure that he knows."

Even though the Assistant U.S. Attorney talked about the father in the past tense ("your father knew"), the son used present tense language in referring to his father ("he knows"). If the son believed his father was dead, he would have said, "I don't know for definite that he knew. I would guess that he probably did know. I don't know for sure that he knew." His present tense language told us he knew his dad was alive. We eventually found the father alive and well living in Costa Rica. He was extradited back to the United States, sentenced, and sent to prison.

While deception is usually found when people use present tense verbs, past tense language can sometimes reveal a person is being dishonest. We often see this in a missing person case. Statistics show that when a person vanishes often times a family member or someone close to the victim is responsible for the person's disappearance. When a family member or a friend talks about the missing person in the past tense he is revealing that he knows the person is dead or that he believes the person is dead. We saw this with the Susan Smith case. Before she confessed to drowning her two boys, she stated, "My children wanted me. They needed me and now I can't help them."[7] She should have stated that her children want her and need her since she should be holding out hope they are still alive. By using past tense verbs *wanted* and *needed*, she was telling everyone listening she knew her children were dead.

We saw the same thing with Scott Peterson when his wife Laci disappeared. On December 24, 2002, Laci Peterson, who was eight months pregnant, vanished from her Modesto, California neighborhood. Scott Peterson told the police he last saw his wife that morning as she left their house to walk their dog. He then left to go fishing at the Berkeley Marina. When he returned home Laci was gone. An intense search was conducted but Laci was not found. Peterson soon became a suspect in his wife's disappearance. He gave several interviews proclaiming his innocence. In January 2003, he was interviewed by Diane Sawyer on the ABC show *Good Morning America*.

Sawyer: "What kind of marriage was it?"

Peterson: "God, the first word that comes to mind is, you you know, glorious. I mean we took care of each other, very well. She was amazing. She is amazing."[8]

At the time Peterson gave this interview, Laci had not been found. Yet he refers to his wife in the past tense, "She was amazing." It appears he realized what he had said so he tried to correct it and act as if she is still alive by stating, "She is amazing." However, his words had already betrayed him. He told the whole nation on national television that he knew his wife was dead.

On April 13, 2003, a baby's body, with his umbilical cord still attached, surfaced on the northern California shoreline about three miles north of the Berkeley Marina. The next day a woman's body was discovered near the same location. DNA tests would later identify the bodies as Laci Peterson and her baby. On April 18, 2003, Scott Peterson was arrested in connection with the death of his wife. On November 12, 2004, Scott Peterson was found guilty of murdering his wife Laci and his unborn son Conner.

On August 11, 2009, 38-year-old Kristi Cornwell went for an evening stroll near her home in Blairsville, Georgia. As Cornwell was walking down Jones Creek Road she was talking on her cell phone to her boyfriend Douglas Davis. According to Davis, Cornwell said that a car was approaching her. Davis then heard what he thought was a struggle and Cornwell yelling for help. Davis contacted the police but Kristi Cornwell was no where to be found. It appeared she had been kidnapped while walking down the road.

On August 20, 2009, Douglas Davis appeared on NBC's *Today Show*. In his interview with Ann Curry he stated the following:

> "Well it is tragedy. You know someone as precious as this woman you know Kristi loved life, she loved to laugh, and she really deserves to come home. She has an awesome family whom she loves dearly. She has a wonderful son and (unintelligible) his mother. And I believe that this tragedy can come to a happy ending. I believe she's still alive."[9]

Twice Davis talks about Cornwell using past tense language; "Kristi loved life, she loved to laugh." He does the same thing when he appeared on the *Nancy Grace* show which aired on August 24, 2009 on CNN. Davis told Nancy Grace that before she was abducted Cornwell mailed him a devotional book that he has been reading every day. He then stated the following:

> "I don't let it out of my sight. It's such a treasured gift. And this is who Kristi was. She liked to give. She really enjoyed life. She's a very intelligent woman and a loving mother. A dear sister to her brother Richard. She loved her mom and her dad. Her family."[10]

Davis talks about Cornwell in the past tense when he says, "And this is who Kristi was. She liked to give. She really enjoyed life. . . She loved her mom and her dad." Talking about Cornwell as if she is no longer alive is an indication that Davis knows Cornwell is dead. Another possible and more probable explanation for his language is that despite his statements that he believes she is still alive; he actually believes she is dead. This is based on what he heard on his cell phone. The fact that one week had gone by and no one had heard from Cornwell points to her not being alive. He does not want to admit that things do not look good and he wants to maintain a degree of hope. However, his true feelings are revealed when he uses past tense language.

On January 1, 2011, Richard Cornwell, the brother of Kristi Cornwell, discovered a partially buried skeleton nine miles from where his sister disappeared. Several days later a medical examiner confirmed that these were the remains of Kristi Cornwell. The primary suspect in her murder, James Scott Carringer, killed himself in April 2010 when police tried to arrest him for kidnapping and raping a Kennesaw State University student. Unfortunately, we may never know for certain who killed Kristi Cornwell.

Leah Freeman was a 15 year old girl living in Coquille, Oregon. On June 28, 2000, her boyfriend, Nick McGuffin, dropped Leah off at the home of her best friend Sherrie Mitchell. McGuffin told Leah he would be back at 9:00 p.m. to pick her up. When McGuffin returned to Sherrie's house at 9:00 that night Sherrie told him that she had gotten into an argument with Leah. Leah had just left and was walking home. McGuffin claims he drove around Coquille looking for Leah but he never found her. Even though several people saw her walking around town Leah never made it home. The next morning her mother reported her missing. About one month later, Leah Freeman's body was found in the woods several miles outside of town.

As the police conducted their investigation they had a suspect in their sites. It was Leah's boyfriend Nick McGuffin. McGuffin had been acting strangely in the hours and days after Leah's disappearance. He became a prime suspect when he failed a polygraph test. Despite their suspicions, the police could not gather enough evidence to charge McGuffin with Leah's murder. The case would go unsolved for ten years.

In August 2008, the town of Coquille hired Mark Dannels as their new police chief. With pressure coming from the community and the Freeman family, Dannels reopened the Leah Freeman murder investigation. In addition to interviewing hundreds of witnesses, the authorities also turned to the Vidocq Society for assistance. The Vidocq Society is a group of professionals who apply their skills and experience to cold case homicides and unsolved deaths. By donating their time, deductive reasoning, and forensic talents, they help to solve the unsolved cases they receive. In November 2009, the Vidocq Society asked me to analyze the statement McGuffin gave to the police shortly after Leah disappeared. As I reviewed his statement I could see there were several signs he was being deceptive about what happened the night Leah went missing. I shared my findings with the Vidocq Society and with the ABC show *20/20* who was doing a story on the unsolved murder. I discussed with correspondent Jim Avila the verb tenses McGuffin used. In talking about Leah Freeman and Sherrie Mitchell's friendship, McGuffin stated, "Sherrie is like was like her best friend."[11] McGuffin used past tense language in stating that Sherrie and Leah are no longer best friends. The question is how does he know the friendship had ended? At the time he gave this statement, Leah was still missing. This means he may have talked to Leah while she was missing and she told him Sherrie was no longer her best friend. A more plausible explanation for his past tense verbiage is that he knows Leah is dead. Since he killed her or witnessed her death, he knows that she and Sherrie are no longer best friends.

In August 2010, a Coos County, Oregon grand jury indicted Nick McGuffin for the murder of Leah Freeman. McGuffin was arrested and bail was set at $2 million. He pled not guilty and went to trial in July 2011. On July 19, 2011, the jury found him guilty of manslaughter. McGuffin was sentenced on August 1, 2011 to ten years in prison for the death of Leah Freeman.

We see the use of past tense language in the disappearance of 5-year-old Haleigh Cummings from Putnam County, Florida. Ronald Cummings, father of the missing girl, claims that someone entered his mobile home during the early morning hours of February 10, 2009 and took Haleigh from her bed. Cummings was at work when the kidnapping occurred. Haleigh was at home with Cummings's girlfriend Misty Croslin. Croslin told the police that she woke up in the middle of the night and discovered the back door was open and Haleigh was gone.

A month would pass and Haleigh's whereabouts were still unknown. In the midst of her disappearance, Cummings and Croslin announced they were getting married. Many people questioned why they would take such a big step while Haleigh was still missing. On March 9, 2009, Croslin spoke to the media about the pending marriage.

"Everybody is probably going to take this marriage thing the wrong way. This is what Haleigh wanted. She has always talked about it, and even if she's not with us, she is still with us."[12]

Croslin referred to Haleigh in the past tense when she said, "This is what Haleigh wanted." If Haleigh was still alive, wouldn't she still want them to tie the knot? If Croslin believed Haleigh was alive, she would have phrased her statement "This is what Haleigh wants."

On March 12, 2009, Cummings and Croslin were married in a small private ceremony. The newlyweds spent their honeymoon in New York City. The next day they appeared on NBC's *The Today Show*. Meridth Viera asked them why it was important to get married at this time. Ronald Cummings responded with the following statement.

"I don't know. I think that my little girl would have wanted it. I would have rather have her to have been there. So obviously when we get her back we will do a much larger and better wedding."[13]

Ronald Cummings also talked about his daughter in the past tense when he said that Haleigh, "would have wanted" them to get married. If he believed his daughter was still alive, he would have phrased his statement "I think that my little girl wants this." Referring to a missing person in the past tense is a strong indication the person knows the missing person is dead.

On September 24, 2010, Ronald Cummings was sentenced to 15 years in prison for selling prescription drugs. On October 8,

2010, Misty Croslin was sentenced to 25 years in prison for her part in drug trafficking. Haleigh Cummings is still missing.

If you want to detect deception, examine all of the verb tenses. If the person is recalling an event, he should be speaking in the past tense. Look to see if the subject uses any present tense verbs. This is an indication the person is not drawing his story from memory but is currently constructing it. Listen to how a person answers a question. If the subject is asked a question that spans his entire life, he should give an answer that accounts for his lifetime. Lastly, when dealing with a disappearance watch for those people who use past tense language. Talking about a missing person in the past tense is a sign they know or believe the person is dead.

CHAPTER 7

Words and Phrases That Indicate Untruthfulness

To make their statement or answer sound believable, deceptive people will sometimes use words and phrases they believe emphasize their truthfulness. However, it has just the opposite effect. Many interviewers have noted that when people use these words and phrases they are being deceptive. The following is a list of some of the more common deceptive sayings.

"I swear on my mother's grave"
"I swear on the Bible"
"God as my witness"
"To tell the truth"
"I swear to God"
"Honest to God"
"To be honest"
"Believe me"
"To be sure"
"Honestly"
"Frankly"
"Really"

If you have conducted a lot of interviews, you probably have a few more sayings you could add to this list. Since a truthful person is being honest, he does not have to convince the interviewer of his truthfulness. Therefore, a truthful person will generally not use these words and phrases. On the other hand, a deceptive person knows he is telling a lie. In the back of his mind, he is thinking the interviewer may not believe him. In order to persuade the interviewer he is being truthful, he may use some additional words to bolster his statement.

I have always been a fan of professional football. Since I grew up in Ohio, I am a die hard Cleveland Browns fan. Another team that I like to watch is the Oakland Raiders. Their black and silver uniforms make them look tough and they play tough. I remember in 1982 when the late Al Davis, the owner of the Raiders, moved the team from Oakland, California to Los Angles. Referring to them as the Los Angeles Raiders did not have the same appeal. In 1995, there was speculation the team might move back to Oakland. On June 22 of that year, owner Al Davis was asked if he was going to move his team from Los Angeles to Oakland. Davis responded, "I don't know what's going on so help me God."[1] The next day, June 23, Davis signed the paperwork sending the Raiders back to Oakland. Did Al Davis know what was going on? Of course he did. He was the owner of the team. We also know that he knew what was going on by his use of the phrase "so help me God." If Davis would have said, "I don't know what's going on" that would have been a good answer. It is still hard to believe but it could be true. However, Davis knew he was close to signing an agreement to send the team back to Oakland. Therefore, in an effort to make his statement sound believable he (perhaps unknowingly) added the phrase, "so help me God" to his statement.

On January 2, 2004, an Ohio woman claimed she had bought the winning Mega Millions lottery ticket worth $162 million but she lost the ticket. Elecia Battle said she purchased the winning ticket at a suburban Cleveland convenience store. As she left the store she dropped her purse in the parking lot and several items fell out including the ticket. She thought she had picked up the ticket and put it back into her purse. The next day when she went to check her numbers she realized the ticket was not in her purse. News of the missing ticket had fortune seekers scouring the parking lot and nearby dumpsters. When interviewed by the media, Battle gave the following statement.

"I do recall all the numbers. They are all somehow family related. No one can tell me what I did and did not play. I did it honestly and I have no doubt."[2]

Battle tries to convince us that she is being truthful by using the word *honestly*. However, the use of this word indicates she is being deceptive. On January 8, 2004, Battle admitted she fabricated the story of losing the winning lottery ticket. She apologized stating, "I'm not a bad person. I'm really not."[3] Even in her apology she used the word *really* which is a word that indicates untruthfulness. "I'm not a bad person" is a good statement. Adding the phrase, *I'm really not* indicates the person has not always been good. Battle's criminal history shows she has been arrested for assault, criminal trespassing, and credit card fraud. The police then added one more charge to her rap sheet, filing a false police report.

In the previous chapter, we looked at the verb tenses Ronald Cummings and Misty Croslin used in their statements regarding the disappearance of Cumming's daughter Haleigh. Two days after Haleigh vanished Cummings and Croslin were interviewed by Greta Van Susteren on the Fox News show *On The Record with Greta Van Susteren*. When questioned about how often they use the back door to their mobile home, Croslin responded, "We really do not use the back door."[4] Croslin wants to give the impression they never use the back door but the word *really* indicates they do use it. This was later confirmed in the interview when Croslin provided additional information. "Once in a while I will take the garbage out through the back door or leave through the back door and take a vacuum and vacuum the car out but that is the only time we use the back door."[5]

I recently watched the show *The Interrogators* which airs on the BIO Channel. This program focuses on real-life crimes and shows seasoned investigators interviewing suspects. The episode that I watched centered on the murder of four homeless men in South Bend, Indiana. On January 9, 2007, their bodies were discovered in an abandon building known as "The Fort" where numerous homeless men lived. The police interviewed Randy Reeder who was also homeless and had stayed at "The Fort." During the interview, we find the following questions and answers.

    Question: "When was the last time you were in that building?"
    Reeder: "I don't know. I really couldn't tell you. It's been a couple of months or so."

Question: "Who and why do you think somebody would do this to those four men?"

Reeder: "I really don't know. They didn't have nothing, you know? I don't know, you know. Really."[6]

Despite using the word *really* three times, Reeder convinces the detectives that he does not know anything about these murders. Reeder tells them another man who lived in "The Fort" off and on was Dan Sharp. The detectives interview Sharp and notice that his boots match a bloody boot print found at the crime scene. They then give Sharp a polygraph. After he fails the test, he admits that he killed the four men because they took some of his belongings. He also tells them that Randy Reeder helped him in the killings. Sharp was arrested as well as Reeder. On August 6, 2007, Reeder went on trial for participating in the murders. Several days later he was found guilty. On September 7, 2007, Reeder was given the maximum sentence of 260 years. As part of a plea agreement, Dan Sharp was sentenced to 65 years.

In 1994, Gulf County Florida Sheriff Al Harrison was accused by several female inmates of forcing them to perform oral sex on him in exchange for favors such as being appointed to the position of trustee at the jail, or receiving passes which allowed them to go home for the holidays. It was alleged that the sheriff's sex for special treatment program had been going on since 1989. At his trial, Harrison told the jury, "I swear to God I ain't never touched no inmate."[7] You have heard of double negatives. Here we have a triple negative with the words *ain't*, *never* and *no*! That alone would raise suspicion about his statement. More importantly the sheriff uses the phrase, "I swear to God." In an effort to convince the people of Gulf County that he was innocent, the sheriff resorts to using a phrase that indicates untruthfulness. To Sheriff Harrison, his statement is a truthful statement. After all, he was not charged with rape. In his mind, he did not do any of the touching. Harrison was convicted of violating the civil rights of an inmate and in March 1995 he was sentenced to federal prison for a term of four years and three months.

In April 2010, comedian Sarah Silverman published the book *The Bedwetter: Stories of Courage, Redemption, and Pee.* In her book, Silverman talks about her struggles with bedwetting which continued into her high school years. She also discusses the depression she suffered because of her years of bedwetting. On May 24, 2010, Silverman posted the following statement on her Twitter account: "I swear to god I'm going to murder my dog if more people don't buy my book right now." I am sure most people do not believe Silverman was seriously considering murdering her dog. She is an edgy comedian and this type of statement fits her personality. Even if you know nothing about Silverman, her use of the phrase "I swear to God" tells you she had no intention of killing her dog.

In chapter one, I talked about former Illinois Governor Rod Blagojevich who was convicted of charges related to trying to sell Barack Obama's senate seat. In responding to his conviction, Blagojevich told the press, "I frankly am, am stunned."[8] The word *frankly* is not needed and is a word that indicates untruthfulness. The governor's language tells us he probably was not stunned by his conviction. We see further evidence of this when he hesitates by repeating the word *am*. It is as if he has to pause to think about what he is going to say.

When analyzing these words and phrases you should look to see where in the statement they appear. A suspect may properly deny committing the crime. An interviewer may then challenge him on his denial. This may cause the suspect to use one of these words or phrases that indicate untruthfulness. He may respond by saying, "I swear to God I am telling you the truth." He may be using the deceptive phrase not because he is lying, but because the interviewer does not believe him. He feels he has to convince the interviewer he is telling the truth. However, if the interviewer simply asks a question and the person uses one of these words or phrases it is a stronger indication of deception. The earlier in the statement these words and phrases that indicate untruthfulness appear, the greater the chance the person is lying.

Remember these words and phrases are only an indication of deception. They are not an absolute. Some people may have a habit of using these phrases. In looking for fugitives, I have had people tell me, "Honest to God I don't know where he is." I believed they were being truthful because this was the only indication of deception in their statement.

If you want to detect deception, look for words and phrases that indicate untruthfulness. Remember, the shortest sentence is the best sentence. Additional words give you additional information. A truthful person will usually not try to convince you he is telling the truth because he knows he is being truthful.

CHAPTER 8

Active Voice vs. Passive Voice

Active voice is when the subject performs the action denoted in the verb. In the sentence, "The man ate the hamburger" the man is performing the action of eating the hamburger. In passive voice, the subject is not acting but is being acted upon. In the sentence, "The hamburger was eaten by the man" the subject (the hamburger) is not performing the action but is receiving the action of being eaten. Passive voice is accepted in scientific writings where the emphasis is not on the author but on the process that is occurring; "The two chemicals were mixed in a beaker." Who mixed the chemicals is not as important as the procedure and the outcome of the testing.

Passive voice allows a person to speak or write without mentioning names or using personal pronouns. While this may be acceptable in the scientific community it is not permissible for a person to use passive language when an interviewer is trying to obtain all the information that is available. Passive language allows the interviewee to conceal the identities of those involved.

There are some things that do not happen by themselves. A gun firing, a knife lunging, or a car starting all require someone to perform the action. Deceptive people will sometimes use passive language to avoid telling the interviewer who carried out the act. In chapter four, I talked about the man who said that his wife committed suicide by shooting herself in the head with a pistol. In his written statement that he gave to the police, we find the following portion:

> "She got up off the waterbed and picked the pistol up from her dressing. I think but am not sure. She played with the gun a little and then put it to her temple because she knew people playing with knives or guns made me nervous. She smiled at me and said, 'You don't think I'll do it do you?' I smiled back and told her no I didn't trying to hide my nervousness because I knew that was why she was teasing me in that way. The gun went off. I sat on the bed for about 5 to 10 seconds. I got up and went to where she fell."

We saw deception in this statement because the husband used the word *dressing* and not *dresser*. We then discovered that in the second sentence he qualified his statement by saying he is not sure if that is what happened. Now we see that he used passive language in talking about the gun firing; "the gun went off." He does not tell us who fired the gun. He wants us to believe his wife fired the gun but he does not state that. He does not say, "She then pulled the trigger and the gun went off." The reason he used passive language is because he shot his wife and killed her. It is hard for him to say that she pulled the trigger since that would be a lie. He is not going to state that he shot her because he would be confessing to murder. So, he chose to use passive language and not mention who pulled the trigger. As I previously mentioned, the husband eventually confessed that he shot his wife.

In a similar but opposite type of case, we see passive language in a statement given by a woman who said that her husband shot himself. She wrote that they were having a "very serious discussion" which means they were having an argument. She continues her statement with the following:

> "While talking, I heard a pistol cocked. I looked down and he had the pistol at his side. I asked him what he was doing. He made a statement that I would never trust him again. Then he moved the gun up and it immediately went off and he fell."

Although she states he had the pistol at his side and he moved the gun up presumably towards his head, she does not tell us that he shot himself or that he pulled the trigger. Instead, she uses passive language stating the gun "immediately went off." Guns do not go off by themselves. After analyzing her entire statement, it was quite clear that she shot her husband over his infidelity.

In chapter three, I talked about the late Senator Ted Kennedy's car accident in 1969 on Chappaquiddick Island. His passenger, Mary Jo Kopechne, died in the accident when Kennedy drove his car off the bridge and into Poucha Pond. The following day Kennedy gave the police a statement in which he said, "The car went off the side of the bridge."[1] Earlier in his statement Kennedy admitted he was driving the car. However, when it came time to talk about the accident he used passive language. Cars do not drive themselves. He could have said, "I drove the car off the side of the bridge" which is what happened. However, he did not want to admit to that so he used passive language. To this day, there is speculation as to where the two of them were going, if Kennedy was driving under the influence, and why it took so long for him to report the accident to the police.

In some situations where a person is being deceptive, he may use passive language because the act never occurred. There was a case in which an officer made an arrest and booked the subject into the detention center. Upon searching the subject, the officer discovered the subject had in his possession a large sum of money. The officer claimed that he placed the money in a property locker along with the subject's other belongings. Several days later when the suspect was being released on bond it was discovered that the money was missing from the locker. When we look at the officer's statement about what he did with the money, we find he used passive language; "The money was placed in the property locker." The officer does not tell us who placed the money in the locker. It is difficult for him to state, "I placed the money in the locker" because he did not do it. It turned out the officer didn't put the money in the locker but kept it for himself. It was easier for him to lie using passive language as opposed to active language.

Passive language appeared in the ransom note that was left after JonBenet Ramsey had presumably been kidnapped. In the ransom note, we find the following warning to her parents.

"Speaking to anyone about your situation, such as Police, F.B.I., etc., will result in your daughter being beheaded. If we catch you talking to a stray dog, she dies. If you alert bank authorities, she dies. If the money is in any way marked or tampered with, she dies."[2]

The description of JonBenet being killed is in passive voice. The writer does not tell us who will behead JonBenet. This is especially clear in the phrase *she dies*. Had the writer used active voice he would have written, "We will kill her." The most likely reason why the writer gave a passive threat is because he knows that JonBenet is dead. It is not possible for him to kill her again if the parents do not comply with his wishes.

There is another indicator in this statement that the writer knew JonBenet was dead when the ransom note was written. The phrase *she dies* is in the present tense. The writer should be speaking in the future tense; "she will die." The writer cannot state "she will die" because JonBenet is already dead. The writer states that JonBenet will be beheaded if the Ramseys do not comply with their demands. JonBenet's body was found in the basement of her home. Although she was not beheaded she did have a cord wrapped around her neck. This may have caused the writer to use term *beheaded*.

If you want to detect deception, look to see if the subject is speaking in passive voice. He may be trying to avoid telling you who was involved, or he may be using passive language because he is making up the story. In many deceptive stories, the passive language can be seen when the subject mentions an inanimate object performing a function such as a gun firing. He may not want to tell you who discharged the weapon, or he may not want to admit that he fired the gun.

CHAPTER 9

Order Is Significant

The order in which a person mentions things is important. When a person is stating who was involved or who was present he may mention several names such as "Tony, Jim and I went to the game last night." There is a reason why he listed Tony's name first and Jim's name second. Maybe he likes Tony better than Jim. Maybe he has known Tony longer than he has known Jim. It could also be that Jim is his best friend but it was Tony who invited him to the game which caused him to state Tony's name first. The point is there is a reason why he mentioned the names in a particular order.

My wife Pam has a younger sister named Susan. When Pam and I were married Susan became my sister-in-law. Several years later when Susan married Charlie I then gained a brother-in-law. Whenever I talk about this couple I always refer to them as "Susan and Charlie." I never call them "Charlie and Susan." I do not think about what order I should mention their names. I automatically refer to them as "Susan and Charlie" because I have known Susan longer than I have known Charlie. We do the same thing when talking about our kids. Most people will mention their oldest child first and their youngest child last. This is because the oldest one has been around the longest. If a parent is talking about something pertaining to the youngest child, then he or she may mention the youngest one first and then continue to talk about the rest of their children according to their ages.

There was a case in which a mother and her two children had been shot to death in their garage. The crime scene indicated they had just returned home when someone killed them before they had a chance to exit their car and enter their house. Several days after their bodies were discovered, the father was arrested for murdering his family. In his interview with the police, he made the following statement.

> "I was at a basketball game. I couldn't have killed my wife and our kids. After work today, I went home before the game tonight. I made a telephone call. I left the house about fifteen minutes later. I played basketball until 9:15. I arrived back at the house at 9:22. I arrived at the house and found that somebody murdered my wife and our two children, Jill 5 and Brad 7."

I had mentioned earlier that when talking about their children most people will refer to them from the oldest to the youngest. In his statement, the father reverses the order and names his youngest child first and the older one second, "Jill 5 and Brad 7." There is a reason why he did this. Perhaps he shot Jill first and this caused him to unwittingly mention her name first. When an autopsy was performed on Jill's body it was discovered that she may have been sexually molested. Although the police never charged the father with child molestation some in law enforcement believe he did molest his daughter. Maybe this is why he placed her name before his son's name. Perhaps he felt closer to his daughter than to his son.

Order is also important when mentioning other things in a statement. The subject is giving us additional information by the order he lists things. There was a man who was suspected of selling illegal drugs. He voluntarily submitted to a police interview in which he denied being a drug dealer. During his interview they asked him for his address. This is standard questioning that provides the interviewer with background information on the subject. If they need to get in touch with him at a later date, they now know where he lives. I am not going to reveal his actual address but I will use the same order he used. He told the police that he lived at "1411 West Sand Street, Kendall, FL, apartment 10." According the U.S. Postal Service, the correct way to address an envelope is to first write the person's name, then the street address, apartment or suite number, followed by the city, state and zip code. Most people abide by that format and their mail usually arrives in a timely fashion. Our suspected drug dealer chose to arrange his address in different order. Instead of mentioning his apartment number directly after the street address, he placed it at the very end of the address after the state he lives in. What this tells us is he is trying to distance himself from his apartment. It is a matter of record where he lives. This is not something he can hide so he has to tell them what apartment he resides in. However, since a part of him does not want to tell the authorities where he lives, he unknowingly places his apartment number at the end of the sentence. He does not want to be associated with his residence. When the police searched his apartment they didn't find any drugs but they found illegal firearms. Now we know why he listed his apartment number at the end of the address.

I once was given a letter to analyze that was addressed to the parents of a female college student who had been murdered. The letter was written by a man who attended the same college as the victim. In the letter, he was expressing his condolences in the loss of their daughter. As I read the letter it became apparent to me this man was infatuated with the deceased woman. There were several things in the letter that pointed to this and one of them had to do with order. In describing their daughter, he wrote, "She was one of the few gifted people that possessed beauty, intelligence, strength, and courage." There are four attributes he said this young lady possessed: beauty, intelligence, strength and courage. To him, the most important characteristic she possessed was her beauty. We can surmise this because that is what he listed first. The fact that she was beautiful was more important to him than her other traits of being intelligent, strong and courageous. The investigator confirmed this telling me that her friends said she wanted nothing to do with this guy.

The day that O.J. Simpson failed to turn himself into the Los Angeles Police Department, his friend, Robert Kardashian, read for the media a letter written by Simpson. The letter would become known as the "suicide letter" because in it Simpson said goodbye to many of his friends. In his letter, Simpson talked about how he loved his ex-wife Nicole Brown Simpson. He admitted they had problems in their relationship but he said things were not as bad as the media made it out to be.

> "Unlike what's been in the press, Nicole and I had a great relationship for most of our lives together. Like all long term relationships we had a few downs and ups."[1]

Look at the last sentence. Simpson states they had a few "downs and ups." How would you phrase that statement? Chances are you would say, "ups and downs." Most people mention ups first because they like to think they have more ups in their lives than downs. Although he tries to deny it, Simpson unintentionally tells us they had more downs in their relationship than ups. That is what the battered photographs and the 911 calls would indicate. The order in which he described their "downs and ups" showed us his true feelings.

Some of the old wanted posters from the 1800's have the headline, "Wanted: Dead or Alive." The emphasis was on bringing the bandit in dead because in some cases that was the easiest way to capture him. We see similar use of this language in the case of missing pilot Lt. Commander Scott Speicher. Lt. Speicher was the first casualty of the Persian Gulf War. On January 16, 1991, his F/A-18 Hornet was shot down over Western Iraq during the first night of Operation Desert Storm. It was unknown if Lt. Speicher survived the crash so he was listed as "Missing in Action." When the Gulf War ended Lt. Speicher's status was changed to "Killed in Action / Body Not Recovered." In 2001, the CIA released a report that said Lt. Speicher may have survived the crash by ejecting. In 2002, the Pentagon the changed his status to "Missing / Captured." The uncertainty of Lt. Speicher's survival and the constant changing of his status prompted a Pentagon official to state he was "not sure if Scott Speicher is dead or alive." Based on the language and its order, we can conclude the Pentagon believed Lt. Speicher was dead. If Pentagon officials believed there was a strong possibility he was still alive, they probably would have said they are not sure if he is "alive or dead." On August 2, 2009, Lt. Speicher's remains were found in the desert in Iraq. It appears that he died during the crash and was never captured. It was reported that a desert-dwelling group called the Bedouins buried his body.

The order in which a person mentions things not only provides us with additional information but it can sometimes show us if a person is being deceptive. This occurs when a person gives us a statement that is out-of-order. When a person gives a truthful statement he is recalling from memory what happened. He will list the events in chronological order as he mentally relives the incident. When a person is making up a story there will be certain parts he does not have a memory to rely upon as he states what happened. Therefore, he may make an out-of-order statement. He may mention something that is out of sequence. We see this in the statement given by a delivery driver who claimed he was robbed while on his route. In chapter two, we saw this driver used the unique word *standing* in reference to a truck that was blocking his path. He also used the unique number *three* in reference to how many men robbed him. As we look at his statement again we see that he mentions something that is out-of-order.

> "I loaded my truck and left the store. When I stopped at Spring Avenue and 5th street I was assaulted by three men with weapons. Earlier in the day I saw a truck parked at Spring Avenue and 5th street. As I left the store I saw the same truck standing in front of me preventing me from passing. When I tried to pass the truck two men opened the door to my truck and pointed their weapons at me."

The subject starts out saying he loaded his truck and left the store. While he was stopped at an intersection he was assaulted by three men. Instead of moving forward in his story, he then backs up in time and states, "Earlier in the day I saw a truck parked at Spring Avenue and 5th street." This statement is out-of-order because it occurred before the incident which he has already mentioned. Had he been telling this story from memory he should have first stated he saw a suspicious truck parked on the street and then talk about how the men in this truck robbed him later in the day. The subject was quick to state that he was robbed. He then realized he needed to set the stage for this crime so he digressed and stated that he saw the robber's truck earlier in the day. As I had mentioned this was an inside job. The truck driver knew the robbers and participated in the theft. Because there were parts of the story in which he was not being completely truthful, this caused him to have an out-of-order statement.

In chapter six, I talked about the father who disappeared in a scuba diving accident several days before he was to be sentenced for income tax evasion. We saw that his son talked about his dad in the present tense even though his dad was allegedly dead. When I analyzed the son's statement I found further signs he was being deceptive about the supposed accident. According to the son, he and his father went diving around an oil rig. While under water they split up and agreed to meet at a certain spot in five minutes. When the son returned to the location his father was not there. The son waited for a couple of minutes but his dad did not show up. The son then surfaced and asked two men on their boat if his father was with them. They responded they had not seen his dad. The son then dove again looking for his dad. He described his search in the following way.

> "I descended again to look for him. By now I only had about 300# of air. I only had enough air to search for a minute. I looked but did not see him anywhere. I was forced to surface because I was about out of air. I started the dive with about 2000# of air. I asked my dad if he had enough air to make the dive and he said yes. After I surfaced the second time he had still not come up. I could not go down anymore because I was out of air with only 75# left."

As you read the son's statement look at the order in which the events occurred. There is one thing that is out-of-order. After the father has run out of air and has presumably drowned, the son tells us he spoke to his dad; "I asked my dad if he had enough air to make the dive and he said yes." The son mentions this because he wants us to know that he and his father had the same amount of air. This is important because if the son is out of air then the father must also be empty and therefore most likely dead. Had this been a truthful story that was coming from memory, the son would have mentioned this fact earlier in his statement. Perhaps when they first entered the water he could have told us they both had 2,000 pounds of air. That too would have set the stage for this drowning. This out-of-order statement tells us the son knows his father is alive. It also tells us the son has spoken with his father in the time period between the alleged drowning and when he wrote his statement. The reason the son slips up is because to him his story makes sense. He knows his dad is alive and he has spoken with him. Therefore, it goes unnoticed by him that he mentions talking to his dad after his dad has supposedly drowned. As I stated earlier we eventually found the father and arrested him.

If you want to detect deception, take a look at the order in which the subject lists names, things, and events. There may be some information to be gained by the order in which things are mentioned. Out-of-order statements are an indication of deception. It is a sign the subject may not be recalling his story from memory. He may have forgotten to tell you something that he believes is important for his story to sound believable. Therefore, he has to back up in his story and insert the additional information.

CHAPTER 10

Personal Dictionary

Everyone has their own personal dictionary. By that I mean, certain words mean certain things to people. Some people may refer to a firearm as a "gun" while others may call it a "pistol." Some people may refer to an automobile as a "car" while others may call it a "vehicle." Everyone has their own unique language.

One of the rules in Statement Analysis is that there are no synonyms. Every word means something different. In some cases, the meaning may only be slightly different but nonetheless different. When you see the word *girl* what do you picture? Some people may picture a cute five-year-old. Others may picture a ten-year-old. Still, others may have a vision of a fifteen-year-old. When some people see the word *girl* they may picture her with brown hair. Others may envision her with blond hair. The point is we all have our own definition for the word *girl* and no two people share the exact same definition. When you see the word *female* what do you picture? You did not visualize the exact same thing as you did for the word "girl" because the words *girl* and *female* do not mean the same thing to you. The same is true for the words *woman* and *lady*. All four of these words refer to the fairer sex. All four of these words have a different meaning.

In many statements, it can be determined if a person is telling the truth or lying by examining his personal dictionary. In a truthful story, the subject's language will remain consistent. If he views an automobile as a car, he will always call it a car throughout his story. There is no reason for him to call it a vehicle because to him it is a car. Constantly using the same language is an indication the person is giving a truthful statement.

On the other hand, a deceptive person will sometimes change his language when telling a story. Because he is making up the story he may not be personally attached to it and therefore he may not follow his personal dictionary. Instead, he will use synonyms to describe the same thing. One time he may call it a car. Another time he may call it a vehicle and later in his statement he may call it an automobile. This change in language is an indication of deception unless there is a justifiable reason for changing the language. Consider the following story.

> "Last Thursday I got into my vehicle and started to drive to Jacksonville, Florida. As I was driving down Interstate 95 I heard a sound in the right rear of my car. I pulled my vehicle off the highway and onto the shoulder. I got out of my vehicle and saw that I had a flat tire. I opened the trunk of my car and found that my spare tire was flat. I left my car parked on the shoulder and walked to the nearest gas station to use a telephone."

In this statement, the subject interchanges the word *vehicle* with the word *car*. Three times he refers to it as a "vehicle" and three times he calls it a "car." Because he jumps back and forth between these two words, this makes it highly unlikely there is a justifiable reason for changing the language. This would be an indication he is making up the story. Let's look at this same story but worded slightly different. In this version, the subject changes his language but there appears to be a justification for the change.

> "Last Thursday I got into my car and started to drive to Jacksonville, Florida. As I was driving down Interstate 95 I heard a sound in the right rear of my car. I pulled my car off the highway and onto the shoulder. I got out of my car and saw that I had a flat tire. I opened the trunk of my vehicle and found that my spare tire was flat. I left my vehicle parked on the shoulder and walked to the nearest gas station to use a telephone."

In this second story, the subject consistently refers to his automobile as a "car" until he gets to the end of the statement. In the last two sentences, he calls it a "vehicle." In this case, there is a justified reason for changing the language from car to vehicle. As soon as the car becomes disabled he refers to it as a vehicle. His personal dictionary is that the word *car* means it is operable and the word *vehicle* means it is disabled. We do not know this for certain. However, the fact that he only changed his language once and this changed occurred at a logical point within the statement would indicate a justification for the change.

In 1995, Mark and Donnah Winger lived in Springfield, Illinois. In June of that year, they started a family by adopting a baby girl whom they named Bailey. Life seemed good for the Wingers. However, a few months later Donnah Winger would be murdered in her own home. On August 29, 1995, Mark Winger told the police he was in the basement of their home running on a treadmill when he heard a commotion upstairs. He said he went upstairs to see what was going on and found Bailey alone in the master bedroom. Hearing sounds coming from the dining room Winger stated, "I just grabbed my gun and started going down the hall."[1] As he approached the dining room he saw Donnah on the floor with a man on top of her clubbing her with a hammer. Winger shot the intruder in the head stating, "When I came down the hallway I had my weapon pointed at him and I went to pull the trigger."[2] He then called 911. Unfortunately, his wife Donnah died at the hospital without regaining consciousness. The intruder, who was later identified as Roger Harrington, was also dead. Mark Winger was seen as a hero; a man defending his family and his home. It seemed like an open and shut case especially when it was discovered that Harrington had been a psychiatric patient and had a history of delusions. However, when we look at Mark Winger's statements we have a problem. Let's look again at his two statements.

"I just grabbed my gun and started going down the hall."

"When I came down the hallway I had my weapon pointed at him and I went to pull the trigger."

First, we see there is a change in language. Winger used the term "gun" and then within a very short time period called it a "weapon." The words *gun* and *weapon* do not mean the same thing. It is very unlikely that while walking down the hall he swapped firearms. So, why did he change his language from gun to weapon? In a short statement such as these two sentences, it can be difficult to find a justification if one does exist. We do not have much information to compare the language with what was going on. I have seen statements written by police officers in which they referred to their firearm as a gun while pursing a suspect. When they shot at a suspect they then call it a weapon. Once the shooting stopped it became a gun again. This change in language makes sense because the word *gun* means it is in their holster or it is in their hand. The word *weapon* means they are discharging the firearm. Once they stop shooting they go back to calling it a gun. In both of Winger's statements, he is doing the same thing; he is going down the hall. Therefore, we would expect his language to remain constant. When he used the word *weapon* he had not yet discharged it but only had it pointed at the intruder. This would be an indication he is not following his personal dictionary and is making up the story.

The second problem with his statement is his language "and I went to pull the trigger." People mean exactly what they say. In this statement, Winger has not told us that he shot Roger Harrington. All he said is that he thought about pulling the trigger. He considered pulling the trigger. This is a big verbal blunder that paints a different picture than the one he wants us to believe. It is easy to miss this because the physical evidence shows Winger did indeed shoot Harrington. However, his language shows he did not shoot him while walking down the hall.

When we consider the unjustified change in language and the words that he used to describe the shooting, we see that Winger was being deceptive. The problem was no one saw his deception. As I mentioned, for several years he was seen as a hero. Then information surfaced that Winger had an affair with his wife's best friend. The police now had a possible motive why Winger would want his wife killed. Based on this new information the case was reopened. The detectives then found photographs of the crime scene that were taken by the first responders. They never saw these photos during their original investigation. The photographs showed the positioning of the bodies which contradicted what Winger had told them. A note found in Harrington's car with Mark Winger's name, address, and a time now indicated to the police that perhaps Harrington had an appointment to meet Winger at his residence. In August 2001, Mark Winger was arrested for the murder of Donnah Winger and Roger Harrington. The police believe that Winger lured Harrington to his home and shot him while he was seated at the dining room table. When Donnah came into the dining room to see what had happened Mark Winger beat his wife to death with a hammer. Winger was found guilty of both murders and was given a life sentence.

Let's look again at the statement given by a man who said that his wife committed suicide by shooting herself in the head.

"She got up off the waterbed and picked the pistol up from her dressing. I think but am not sure. She played with the gun a little and then put it to her temple because she knew people playing with knives or guns made me nervous. She smiled at me and said, 'You don't think I'll do it do you?' I smiled back and told her no I didn't trying to hide my nervousness because I knew that was why she was teasing me in that way.

The gun went off. I sat on the bed for about 5 to 10 seconds. I got up and went to where she fell."

In chapter four, I talked about the unusual language the husband used when he stated that his wife picked the pistol up from her "dressing." We also saw that he did not commit to his statement when he stated, "I think but am not sure." In chapter eight, we saw that he used passive language in reference to the gun discharging; "the gun went off." When we look at his statement again we see that he used two different words to describe the firearm that killed his wife. He first says she picked up a "pistol." Then he says she played with the "gun." The words *pistol* and *gun* do not mean the exact same thing. It does not appear that she changed firearms so why does he change his language? It is because he is making up the story. He does not follow his own personal dictionary. When we look at his language, unusual language, passive language and his personal dictionary, it is easy to see the deception in his statement.

Several years ago I was working a carjacking trial in Elizabeth City, North Carolina. The defendant, Antoine, along with his partner, Gary, had stolen a car from an elderly man who was parked at a Hardee's restaurant. Gary was tried in a separate trial and was found guilty. It was now Antoine's turn to face the music. In a strategic move, Antoine's attorney subpoenaed Gary to testify for the defense. Gary took the stand and admitted that he committed the crime. He also testified that Antoine was not involved but it was another person by the name of Trey who helped him carjack the old man. Since Gary had already been convicted of committing this crime, he figured he would take the blame and try and get his partner Antoine off the hook.

After Gary testified, the judge recessed for the day. The Assistant U.S. Attorney who was prosecuting the case asked me what I thought of Gary's testimony. I told him that despite being a hard core criminal Gary's testimony sounded believable. In fact, ninety nine percent of his testimony was truthful. However, I could tell he was lying when he named Trey as his partner in crime. The prosecutor asked me how I knew that. I shared with him that Gary started off his testimony stating that his co-conspirator was a person named Trey. After that, he never mentions the name Trey again. In referring to Trey, he made the following statements.

> "My partner and I got into the car."
> "I got into the front seat and the other guy got in the back."
> "The individual with me held the gun on the old man."
> "The gentleman in the back seat told me where to drive."

Gary uses four different synonyms to refer to his cohort. He calls him a "partner," "guy," "individual" and "gentleman." If he viewed Trey as his partner, he should always refer to him as his partner unless there is a justification for changing the language. It is hard to imagine a justifiable reason for changing the language so many times. In this case, the reason for the change is because he is lying about the identity of his partner. Notice that all of his statements are true. The guy did get into the back seat of the car. The individual did possess a gun. However, he does not name who this person was. As I said, his only lie was naming Trey as his partner and not Antoine.

I told the prosecutor that it will be difficult to explain to the jury during closing arguments the concept of a personal dictionary and changes in language. However, what he could tell them is that when the defense attorney asked Gary who committed this crime Gary stated it was Trey. After that, Gary never mentions the name Trey. He refers to him as my partner, the individual, the gentleman, the guy but never again calls him Trey. If Trey was his partner, why wouldn't he continually refer to him as Trey? Why did he use the name Trey only one time? It is because he is lying about who was with him the night he committed this crime. It is difficult for him to continually lie and use the name Trey. The prosecutor did use this argument during his closing. Several of the jurors were shaking their heads agreeing with the prosecutor as he spelled this out. After deliberating for a couple of hours, they found Antoine guilty of carjacking.

In October of 2003, Michelle "Angie" Yarnell of Ivy Bend, Missouri went missing. When the police interviewed her husband, Michael Yarnell, he said that a month earlier Angie told him she had been seeing another man but that the affair had ended. Michael and Angie talked about separating but continued to live together. On October 25, 2003, Michael came home and found that Angie was gone and some of her personal belongings were missing. Yarnell told the police he thought Angie ran off with the man she had been seeing. In promoting his theory that she was with this other man, Yarnell gave the following statement.

"Approximately two and one half months ago a friend had mentioned to me that he had seen my wife with another man driving my truck. I did not believe him at that time because one I did not believe my wife would cheat on me and two he insisted that she was driving. I never known my wife to drive or want to learn to drive a stick shift. Last night, I talked with my friend about him seeing my wife with another guy. He said he seen her twice; the time in the truck and another time in the car. He said he did not recognize the man but knew it was not me."[3]

Yarnell uses two different nouns (*man* and *guy*) to describe his wife's alleged lover. It is possible that Michael's friend views this unknown person as a *man* and Yarnell sees him as a *guy*. This would be more plausible if Yarnell was quoting his friend. However, in his statement to the police he does not use quotation marks. He gives the statement in his own language. Therefore, we have to wonder why he changed his language from *man* to *guy* and back to *man*. There were other signs of deception in his statements which indicated Michael Yarnell was making up the story that his wife was having an affair. The police continued to search for Angie Yarnell but after two years no one had heard from her.

To keep the search for her daughter active, Angie's mother, Marianne Asher-Chapman, appeared on the Montel Williams show in September 2005. The week she appeared on the show Michael Yarnell disappeared. Yarnell remained on the run for nearly three years until it was discovered in August 2008 that he was living in Biloxi, Mississippi. Detectives traveled to Biloxi in October 2008 to interview him. That interview led to his arrest on November 5, 2008. Shortly after his arrest, Michael Yarnell admitted that he killed his wife in October 2003 during a fight they had at their Missouri home. He stated he caused Angie's death by pushing her off a 10-foot-high deck at their home. He then drove his wife's body to a boat ramp at the Lake of the Ozarks, loaded her into a canoe and paddled out to an island. Once he reached the island he attempted to get her body onto the island but lost her in the water. Angie's body has never been found.

When small amounts of money disappear from a bank, we can sometimes tell which teller is skimming the money by examining the employee's personal dictionary. In one such instance, a teller gave the following statement.

> "At the end of the day, I counted the currency that was in my drawer. I wrote down the total amount and then counted it a second time as is our practice. I placed the currency in a bag and recorded the total amount. I then put the money in the safe."

The teller starts out using the word "currency" and ends her statement referring to it as "money." The words *currency* and *money* do not mean the exact same thing. A change in language means a change in reality. Something has happened which has caused her to change her language. It is possible that according to her personal dictionary when the cash is in the drawer or in the bag it is called currency. When it is in the safe it is called money. This would then be justification for changing the language. The problem is this justification is not probable. Whether it is in the drawer, the bag or the safe it is still in the possession of the bank. Therefore, we would expect a person to refer to it using the same noun. So why did she change her language? Most people use the word *money* when talking about what is in their purse or wallet. She placed the *currency* in the bag and placed the *money* in her purse. At the end of her statement when she talked about putting it into the safe, she could see herself putting some of it into her purse. Without realizing it, this caused her to change her language and use the word *money* instead of *currency*.

On January 23, 1995, O.J. Simpson went on trial in Los Angeles, California for the murder of his ex-wife Nicole Brown Simpson and her friend Ronald Goldman. That same month he published a book entitled *I Want To Tell You* in an effort to raise money for his defense fund. In his book, Simpson proclaims his innocence.

> "I am one hundred percent not guilty. In my open letter read on television on June 17, 1994 by my friend Robert Kardashian, I said I was innocent. When asked at my arraignment, where the charges against me were first formally stated in court, I said, 'I am one hundred percent not guilty.' I said it again in Judge Ito's chamber and I say it again here."[4]

This sounds like a very strong denial. Most people believe one hundred percent is inclusive of everything. If Simpson is one hundred percent not guilty, then he must be zero percent guilty. However, we must remember that numbers go on for infinity. There are different rating systems that we use. Sometimes we rate things on a scale of one to ten. Other times we rates things on a scale of one to one hundred. So, what scale is Simpson using? What can we learn from Simpson's personal dictionary? Later in his book Simpson talks about his divorce and how Nicole received custody of their two kids. Simpson viewed Nicole as a caring mother and wrote, "I had one thousand percent faith and trust in Nicole's decisions about the kids."[5] We now see that Simpson also rates things on a scale of one thousand. Simpson has more confidence in Nicole's decisions about the kids (1000 percent) than he does in his own innocence (100 percent). Based on his scale of one thousand, Simpson is one hundred percent not guilty of committing murder and nine hundred percent guilty!

In chapter nine, I talked about the husband who was convicted of killing his wife and kids as they sat in their car in their garage. Let's again look at a portion of his statement and examine his personal dictionary.

> "I was at a basketball game. I couldn't have killed my wife and our kids. After work today, I went home before the game tonight. I made a telephone call. I left the house about fifteen minutes later. I played basketball until 9:15. I arrived back at the house at 9:22. I arrived at the house and found that somebody murdered my wife and our two children, Jill 5 and Brad 7."

The man stated that after work he returned "home." After making a telephone call he left his "house." After playing basketball, he arrived back at his "house." He then said he arrived at his "house" and discovered that his family had been murdered. The husband changes his language when he uses the words *home* and *house*. The word *home* indicates a place of warmth and comfort. The word *house* is more cold and sterile. After work, he arrived *home* but after playing basketball he arrived at his *house*. He could have said that after playing basketball he arrived home. His change in language tells us that he knew something was not right at his residence. If he knew or suspected that his family had been killed, this would explain why he used the word *house* and not the word *home*.

Personal dictionaries also apply when a person uses a symbol in lieu of a word. The word *and* is a conjunction that connects two words, phrases, or clauses in a sentence. While it only contains three letters, some people feel the need to take a shortcut when writing a statement and use the ampersand (&) as a substitute for the word *and*. The ampersand does have its place in the English language. It can be used when addressing an envelope to a couple such as "Mr. & Mrs. Jackson." It can be used in corporation names, "Smith & Wesson" and in the names of law firms, "Grant & Jones." It is also used in the titles of books and movies such as "Marley & Me." When analyzing a written statement there is a potential problem if the writer sometimes uses the ampersand and other times uses the word *and*. Remember there are no synonyms in Statement Analysis. Every word means something different. The ampersand and the word *and* do not mean the exact same thing. The same thing applies to the plus sign which some people will use instead of the word *and*. There is a reason why the person changed his language in the statement. It is possible the person was getting tired of writing and chose to use the ampersand or plus sign as a shortcut. If that were the case, we would expect to see these symbols used towards the end of the statement. A potential problem arises if the writer is constantly interchanging the word *and* with these symbols. It is possible that when the person uses the word *and* he is being truthful. When he uses a symbol he is being deceptive. It could also be just the opposite. This is because the writer knows he is about to write a lie or he knows he is withholding information. When his brain sends a signal to his hand to write the statement, it causes him to change his language. We see this change in language in the following portion of a statement given by a woman who said she was sexually assaulted after a night of partying.

> "I arrived at Carol's house around 10:00 p.m. for a party she was having. At round 4:00 a.m., I went to bed in the guest bedroom. At 5:00 a.m., I felt someone lying in bed with me. ~~They~~ He was touching and rubbing me. I moved away from him and he moved closer to me. I rolled over + he put his hand between my legs. When I realized what he was doing I pushed him away and got out of the bed. I then went to Carol's room and told her what happened."

In her statement, the subject uses the word *and* four times. One time she uses the plus sign. The plus sign shows up in the middle of her statement. Previously to using the plus sign she used the word *and* twice. Likewise, after using the plus sign the word *and* appears two times. This would seem to eliminate the idea that she was getting tired of writing the word and chose to use the plus sign as a means to saving time. One possible explanation is that when she uses the word *and* she is telling the truth. He was touching and rubbing her. However, when she exaggerates or in her inebriated state is unsure of what happened she uses the plus sign. Perhaps he put his hands on her leg but not between her legs.

Another explanation for the plus sign is that when she uses the word *and* she is condoning his actions. Even though she says she moved away from him part of her liked the attention she was getting. However, once he places his hand between her legs he has crossed the line. She does not approve of that and it causes her to unknowingly use the plus sign. In this reasoning, the plus sign indicates she strongly objects to something whereas the use of the word *and* means she may go along with it. A change in language means a change in reality. A detective investigating this case would want to find out why she used the plus sign.

Terri Brooks was the assistant night manager at a Roy Rogers restaurant in Fairless Hills, Pennsylvania. On February 4, 1984 around closing time, someone entered the restaurant and stabbed Terri to death. The perpetrator also took $2,500 that was in the restaurant's safe. The next morning an employee found Terri's body. At the time of her death, Terri was engaged to be married to Alfred Keefe. Keefe became a suspect in her murder but there was not enough evidence to charge him with the crime. The case would go unsolved for fifteen years until the police were able to use DNA technology to make an arrest. With Keefe still a suspect, the police were able to get a DNA sample from him when they obtained cigarette butts from his trash. The DNA sample from the cigarette butts matched the DNA found under Terri's fingernails. In February 1999, Alfred Keefe was charged with first-degree murder and robbery. In his written statement to the police, Keefe confessed to killing his fiancée. He began his statement with the following paragraph.

"I went to the restaurant to pick her up, she told me she didn't want to be around me anymore + she hated my guts. I turned away. When I turned around she was holding a kitchen knife. I went toward her and she swung the knife. I grabbed the knife. She came after me. That's all I remember till I got in the car."[6]

In the first sentence, Keefe uses the plus sign as a substitute for the word *and*. When we analyze the language in this first sentence we see he used the word *told* which indicates a strong tone. This makes sense if Terri was adamant that she did not like him and she hated his guts. This first sentence shows signs of being truthful.

When we look at the rest of the statement we find no more plus signs but we see Keefe uses the word *and* one time. An analysis of this part of his statement shows deception and that he is withholding information. Although she has a knife in her hand he states that he went towards her. We would expect him to keep his distance. He then says, "She swung the knife." Notice he does not state in what direction she swung the knife. He does not say, "She tried to stab me." He does not tell us that she missed sticking him with the knife. He then goes on to say that he grabbed not her arm but the knife. One would think he would have cut his hand unless it was a dull knife. He then states that he does not remember anything else until he gets into his car to leave. In an open statement such as this, a person should only tell us what he remembers. When a person says, "I don't remember" he is essentially saying, "I remember that I don't remember." This is a clear sign he remembers something but is choosing not to tell us. Nowhere in this part of his statement or in the rest of his statement does he talk about stabbing Terri. The closest he comes to admitting he injured her is at the end of his statement when he writes, "I didn't want to hurt her."[7]

Based on an analysis of his statement, it may be that when he is telling the truth he uses the plus sign. Maybe she did tell him that she hated his guts. When he is deceptive and is going to withhold information he uses the word *and*. The point is there is a reason why he changed his language. It may or may not have anything to do with deception and we may or may not be able to determine why he altered his words.

We see the same thing with the expression *w/* that is sometimes used as a substitute for the word *with*. They do not mean the exact same thing. The word *with* means one thing and the letter *w* with the forward slash represents something different. If the subject consistently uses one of these throughout his written statement, this would not be a sign of deception but would be insight into his writing style. Most people use the word *with* but there are those that like to use the letter *w* with the forward slash. When both of these show up in a written statement there may be a problem.

In a case of inappropriate conduct, the subject began his statement by writing, "I, John Doe, state that the following is a true account of my conduct w/Jill." The subject starts out using the letter *w* with the forward slash. Towards the end of his statement he writes, "I have not had any improper conduct with Jill in July 2008." The subject now switches language and uses the word *with*. These are the only two times in his statement that he used the *w/* or the word *with*. Both of them are used in conjunction with the name Jill. An analysis of the entire statement concluded that when he used the letter *w* with the forward slash he was being deceptive. He did not give a true account of his actions with Jill. When he used the word *with* he was being truthful. He did not have any improper conduct with Jill in July 2008. His inappropriate behavior occurred before July 2008.

There are other symbols that a person may use in place of a word such as # instead of "number," $ instead of "dollar," % instead of "percent," and @ instead of "at." While these symbols may represent the same thing as their matching word, they do not mean the exact same thing. There is a reason why the person has switched from a word to a symbol or vice versa.

If you want to detect deception, you should look to see if the person has changed his language. Remember that every word and symbol means something different. This even applies to names. William and Bill mean two different things even though they may be referring to the same person. When the subject uses a synonym you need to see if there is a justification for changing the language. Keep in mind there may be a justifiable reason for the change but you cannot find it. Some statements, especially short ones, may not provide you the opportunity to analyze the subject's personal dictionary. The subject may not have used any synonyms. Also, some people may be telling the truth but are purposely using synonyms so their statement does not sound dull. In this case, they are fighting their personal dictionary which wants them to use the same language. Law enforcement officers will often do this when writing a report. They may use the words *suspect* and *subject* throughout their report in referring to the perpetrator. If the only indication of deception is the person used two different words to describe the same thing, you may have to conclude the statement is truthful. It may be you cannot determine why there was a change in language.

CHAPTER 11

Emotions

Not every story will contain emotions. For example, if money is missing from a cash register the employees may be asked to give a statement about what they did the day the money disappeared. Since they are simply accounting for what they did on a particular day, we would not expect to find any emotions within their statement. Stealing money is generally not an emotional event. However, if a subject is describing an unpleasant incident, then emotions will probably appear in his story. In a deceptive story, since there was no incident the subject would not have experienced any emotions. Therefore, a deceptive story may not contain any emotions.

Emotions in a truthful story will usually appear after the incident is over. If a person is suddenly attacked, he usually does not think about getting hurt or being upset as the incident is occurring. Instead, he is thinking about dealing with the situation at hand. The incident is so overwhelming the emotions are suppressed. Once the incident is over and he has time to reflect on what might have happened (injury, loss of life, etc.) he then becomes emotional. That is when a person may start to get the shakes.

After graduating from college, I applied with every federal law enforcement agency that was accepting applications. While I was waiting to get into law enforcement, I took a job working as an Assistant Director for a YMCA camp in Dauphin, Pennsylvania. Camp Shikellamy is situated in the mountains of Dauphin County. The area is full of wildlife including the occasional black bear that may wander into camp. The most prevalent animal is the white-tailed deer. There were so many deer in the area the camp van had deer whistles attached to it in an effort to scare the deer of the road. One night my wife Pam and I were driving back to the camp in our car. As I was driving up a hill I could see the headlights of another car that was coming towards us. I dimmed my headlights and we passed each other at the top of the hill. I then turned my high beams back on and I was surprised to see a deer standing in our lane only a few yards away staring at us. Apparently the deer was on the road when the other car drove by. Because of the close proximity I knew we were probably going to hit the deer. The first thing I thought about was what was this going to feel like. This is because my dad had always told me that hitting a deer is like driving your car into a brick wall. I quickly realized I needed to do something so I tried to swerve around the animal while braking at the same time. I missed the deer but the deer didn't miss us. He decided to run across the road while I was swerving and struck the side of our car. As we came to a stop, he rolled onto our hood and then fell onto the road lying there in front of us. When I got out of the car, he got up and limped into the woods. Our car was still drivable so we continued onto the camp which was only a couple of miles away. Once we got to the camp and I had time to reflect on what had happened, the emotions started to flow. I started to think about what could have happened; how we could have been injured if not killed. Emotions in a truthful statement will appear after the incident is over.

Adam Goldstein, better known as DJ AM, was a popular club disc jockey and musician. On September 19, 2008, he was playing at a college event in Columbia, South Carolina along with Travis Barker the former drummer for the rock group Blink 182. After the show, Goldstein and Barker boarded a Learjet which was bound for Van Nuys, California. Also on board were the pilot and co-pilot, a security guard, and an assistant to Barker. The jet crashed upon takeoff killing everyone except for Goldstein and Barker who were able to escape the flaming fuselage. Goldstein described surviving the crash for *People* magazine.

> "When the plane was on the runway I took my shoes off and fell asleep. The next thing I remember is us crashing into something. I woke up to Travis screaming and the plane engulfed in flames. I remember thinking it was like Miami Vice where a car is on fire and you need to run before the gas tanks explodes – we gotta get out of here. Travis jerked open the door and slid on his butt down a wing that was on fire. I tried to cover my face as I jumped through a fireball. As soon as I hit the ground I remembered 'Stop, drop and roll,' so I started rolling. My eyebrows and layers of my skin were burned off my face. My forehead was gouged and my arm had skin hanging off. I was in shock and didn't feel anything."[1]

There are two emotions in this truthful story. The first one is when Goldstein said that Travis Barker was "screaming." We expect this type of emotion to occur at the peak of the incident. It may have been that Barker was screaming out instructions to exit the plane. Since there is an urgency to leave he uses a loud tone of voice. Barker was also severely injured in the crash. His emotion of screaming may have been a physical response to the pain he was experiencing. When the pain subsides so will the screaming.

The second emotion is one of shock. This type of emotion is based on both physical and mental components. It is this type of emotion that is suppressed and will surface once the incident is over. In Goldstein's statement, he talks about the crash, the flames, exiting the plane, and the injuries he sustained. After mentioning all of this, he then states he was in shock. The placement of his emotion within the story indicates he is telling the truth. Unfortunately for Goldstein, although he survived the plane crash he would die a year later from a drug overdose.

If a person is making up the incident, then there will be no emotions. However, a deceptive person may insert emotions into his story to make it sound believable. What usually occurs is the emotions will be out of place. The subject will place them in his story at the peak of the incident because this is where he thinks they should be. In the case of hitting a deer, a deceptive story may sound something like this.

"As I approached the top of the hill I turned my high beams on. I was surprised to see a deer standing on the road staring at me. I was frightened thinking I was going to hit the deer and damage my car. I slammed on my brakes and attempted to swerve around the deer. The deer hit my right front fender, rolled onto the hood of my car and fell onto the road. By this time I had come to a stop. When I got out of the car the deer got up and limped into the woods. I then got back into my car and drove home."

The first emotion in this story is one of surprise. This is acceptable because it is a brief emotion that only lasts for a few seconds. I am sure you have been in a situation where you thought you were alone when suddenly someone appeared and startled you. The second emotion of being frightened is out of place because it occurs at the peak of the incident. Not only does the subject tell us he was frightened but he tells us why he was frightened; because his car may be damaged. Another indicator the emotions are out of place in this story is the subject never tells us about experiencing any feelings after the incident is over. He never states that after he arrived home he started to tremble or get the chills. He does not mention thinking about what could have happened. This is because he did not experience any emotions since he is making up the story. Therefore, he either forgets to mention any emotions or he places them in the wrong part of his story.

We see out of place emotions in a story given by a woman who said she was robbed while shopping.

"I was leaving Saks in Atlanta and a guy dressed in black from head to toe was in a hooded sweatshirt. I was alone and I was so scared because I had a clutch purse that he wanted."

It would appear the emotion "I was so scared" is located at the peak of the incident. As the robber is trying to grab her purse she is thinking about being scared. We see further signs of deception when she tells us why she was scared, "because I had a clutch purse." She does not fear for her life but fears she may lose her purse. It turned out the woman made up the story of being held up.

In chapter four, I talked about Justin and April Barber who were shot while walking along the beach in St. Augustine, Florida. April died from her wounds and Justin survived. In his statement to the police, Barber described the robber firing the gun.

> "As I stepped in between the man and April, he fired the gun. It was loud. It shocked me. I don't know if the bullet hit me or if it hit April."[2]

Notice where Barber places his emotion of being shocked; it is at the height of the incident. As soon as the gun goes off he tells us that it shocked him. This is different than being surprised. The word *shock* is usually associated with being terrified and has a longer effect on a person. This is our first indication that perhaps things did not happen the way he said they did. Also, look at the language in his statement. After the man fires the gun, Barber states, "I don't know if the bullet hit me or if it hit April." In Barber's mind, there are only two possibilities of where the bullet could have gone. It either hit him or it hit April. In reality, there is a third option. Perhaps the bullet missed the two of them and struck the sand. Bad guys are often bad shots. So, why does Barber assume that when the gun was discharged someone got shot? He can account for every bullet because he pulled the trigger.

As the police conducted their investigation Barber's story did not add up. The robber shot and killed April, a small woman who was of no threat. Yet the robber only wounded Justin who was physically fit and capable of defending himself. Although the robber wanted money he did not take Justin's wallet or any of April's jewelry. After it was discovered that Justin had an affair and had a two million dollar life insurance policy on April, the police believed that Justin killed his wife and staged the robbery scene. In July of 2004, Justin Barber was arrested for killing his wife April. His trial would not take place for almost two years. In June of 2006, he was found guilty of murder. Although the jury recommended he be given the death penalty the judge sentenced him to life in prison.

In chapter eight, I talked about passive language. We looked at a short portion of a statement given by a woman who said that her husband shot himself. She could not state that her husband pulled the trigger so she used passive language and said that the gun "immediately went off." Let's look at some more of her statement.

> "While talking, I heard a pistol cocked. I looked down and had the pistol at his side. I asked him what he was doing. He made a statement that I would never trust him again. Then he moved the gun up and it immediately went off and he fell. At the time I was so shocked I couldn't even remember what actually happened when. The gun went off so fast. He did not

aim or place it on his head it just went off as soon as he motioned it upward."

In addition to the passive language, she adds some emotions to her story; "I was so shocked." We see that she placed the emotions at the peak of the incident. As soon as the gun goes off she becomes "so shocked." The positioning of the emotions within the story would indicate she is being deceptive. We see further signs of deception in that she uses the unique word *actually* when she said, "I couldn't even remember what actually happened when." The word *actually* is used to compare two thoughts. She may be comparing what happened with the lie she is telling. We also see this sentence is fragmented; "what actually happened when." When what? There is some conflict going on in her mind which causes her to not finish her sentence. Lastly, we see that she had a change in language from *pistol* to *gun*. It would appear there is no justification for this change. In this short portion of her statement, we can see several signs of deception. When I analyzed her entire statement there were more indications she was not being truthful about what happened the night her husband died.

If you want to detect deception, pay attention to the emotions in a statement. Look to see if they are genuine feelings by where they are located within the statement. Most people will experience emotions after the incident is over. If the emotions are at the height of the incident, this is an indication the person is making up the emotions and probably making up the story. Remember that most deceptive stories do not have emotions.

CHAPTER 12

Words and Phrases That Span Time

People do not like to lie. This is because most people are raised believing they should always tell the truth. Lying is perceived as being wrong and perhaps even a sin. People also want to be truthful because they know that telling a lie will create internal stress. This stress may surface in the form of a body movement. An interviewer trained to observe nonverbal signals may sense the person is lying. Even a hardcore criminal does not want to lie because he does not know what the interviewer knows. If he tells a lie and the interviewer knows it is a lie, he has just placed his head in the proverbial noose. Therefore, the safest way for a person to play it is to give a truthful statement. This allows him to tell his story with minimal stress and without the fear that his words or actions will betray him.

Although the statement may be truthful, a deceptive person will withhold information that may be incriminating. One way of doing this is to use words or phrases that span time. This type of language allows the subject to skip over something in his story. Many times this goes unnoticed by the interviewer. We see an example of this in the following story.

> "On Saturday, I picked Dan up around 7:30 p.m. and we went to a party at Rob's house. We arrived at Rob's house around 8:00 p.m. There were about twenty people at the party. At 10:00 p.m., we left the party and went to Angelo's restaurant for drinks. Later on we went to Dan's house and watched a movie. The movie was over at 1:00 a.m. I then returned to my residence."

The subject appears to be giving detailed information on what he did that night. However, after going to Angelo's for drinks, the subject uses the phrase *later on* to transition from the restaurant to Dan's house. The subject wants us to believe that after leaving the restaurant they immediately went to Dan's residence. The problem is the phrase *later on* is a vague term. We do not know what time they left the restaurant or what time they arrived at Dan's house. All we know is they left the party at 10:00 p.m. and at 1:00 a.m. the subject returned to his residence. There is a good chance that after leaving the restaurant they did something before they arrived at Dan's house. By using the phrase *later on* the subject avoids mentioning what they did.

There was a midnight security guard who discovered that someone had emptied out the company safe. When the police conducted their investigation, they asked the security guard to write down everything that happened during his shift. In his statement, we find a phrase that spans time.

> "I began to suspect that something was wrong about 3:00 a.m. when I noticed the back gate was unlocked. A few minutes later, I was convinced that something was wrong when I found the payroll office door unlocked and the safe opened."

The security guard skips over something that happened that night when he states "a few minutes later." Even though it may only be a short time period a good investigator would still want to know what was going on during those few minutes. We see another sign of possible deception in the security guard's statement when he gave the time reference of "3:00 a.m." Remember, the number *three* is a liar's number. Maybe it was 3:00 a.m. when he discovered the back gate was unlocked. Then again, maybe he had to come up with a time and the number three popped into his head. As I mentioned, deceptive people do not want to lie and will often tell the truth. The statement that he found the "payroll office door unlocked and the safe opened" is probably a truthful statement. However, notice what he does not tell us. He forgets to mention that the safe was empty. He does not tell us the money was gone. This is because when he saw the safe open the money was still there. It turned out the burglary was an inside job and this security guard was part of the robbery. There is a good chance that during the time period of "a few minutes later" he and his partners were empting the safe.

Lisa Robertson was employed by Quantas Airlines as a flight attendant. On January 24, 2007, she was working a flight that flew from Darwin, Australia to Mumbai, India. On board this flight was actor Ralph Fiennes who has appeared in movies such as *Schindler's List*, *The English Patient*, *The Hurt Locker*, and *Clash of the Titans*. Fiennes had been in Sydney performing a show and was now flying to India as a UNICEF ambassador to promote awareness of HIV and safe sex. Robertson recognized the actor and the two of them struck up a conversation. After the plane landed in India, rumors circulated that Robertson and Fiennes had sex in the plane's bathroom. Robertson denied joining the mile-high club and gave the following statement to her employer.

> "Whilst conversing with Mr. Ficnncs during my break I expressed a need to go to the toilet. I went to the nearby toilet and entered it. He followed me and entered the same toilet. I explained to him that this was inappropriate and asked him to leave. Mr. Fiennes became amorous towards me and after a short period of time I convinced him to leave the toilet which he did. I left the toilet a short time later. At no time did any crew member come to my assistance. At no time were any other customers aware of this incident. At no time did I put the Qantas name or reputation in jeopardy. I consider myself a valuable asset to this company. I deny that my behavior on this flight was such that my employment should be terminated."[1]

Most people would agree her story sounds suspicious. How could Fiennes have entered the bathroom unless she allowed him to enter? In describing being in the bathroom together, we see she uses some language that allows her to skip over something; "After a short period of time I convinced him to leave." I wonder what was going on during that "short period of time." She continues to skip over something and conceal information when she stated, "I left the toilet a short time later." What was she doing during the period she described as "a short time later"?

In examining the rest of her language, we would want to know what she means when she stated Fiennes became "amorous" towards her. She stated that no crew members came to her assistance but she does not tell us why she needed assistance. She never denies the allegations that she had sex with Fiennes in the bathroom. Her only denial is when she stated, "I deny that my behavior on this flight was such that my employment should be terminated." The word *deny* can mean "refuse to accept." If you have a friend who is an alcoholic and he refuses to accept the fact he is an alcoholic, you might say he is in denial. When people use the word *deny* they may be refusing to accept the fact they did something. Robertson refuses to believe her actions are worthy of termination.

We find that Robertson's statement is a truthful statement. Not once does she tell a lie. I believe she did tell Fiennes that it was inappropriate for him to come into the bathroom with her. I believe she did ask him he to leave. I believe they were together in the bathroom for a short period of time and that no customers were aware of what was going on. However, we can clearly see through her use of words that span time she has withheld some information.

Several weeks after giving this statement, Robertson admitted that she did have a passionate fling with Fiennes in the bathroom during the flight. The affair continued at a hotel once they landed in India.

Here is a statement from a man who was shot outside of a nightclub.

"I left the Players Club and was walking to my car. When I got to my car I looked to my right and saw this big guy walking towards me. I think he was in the club but I am not sure. He asked me what my problem was and I told him I didn't have a problem. I turned to get in my car and he tackled me knocking me to the ground. We wrestled on the ground and the next thing I know he had a gun. I tried to grab the gun but he shot me and took off. I then heard someone yell call 911."

The subject uses the phrase *the next thing I know* in regards to the gun appearing in his statement. It would be a smoother transition from wrestling to the gun appearing if he had not used this phrase; "We wrestled on the ground and he had a gun." It could be better worded, "We wrestled on the ground and he pointed a gun at me." The word *and* connects the two actions. By adding the phrase *the next thing I know* the man is skipping over something in his story. It turned out the information he was withholding is that the gun belonged to him. The gun fell out of his waistband when the other man knocked him to the ground. The attacker then picked up the gun and shot the victim with his own gun. The victim does not want to tell the police that he was carrying a gun so he leaves this information out of his story. He wants them to believe the gun belonged to the other man.

When we examine his language we see he referred to the attacker as "this big guy." He used the unique word *this* which indicates closeness because he knows the guy. He alludes to this when he said, "I think he was in the club but I am not sure." We see further evidence he knows his attacker when he said, "We wrestled on the ground." He could have said, "I wrestled with him on the ground." The pronoun *we* always indicates there is a partnership. In this case, their partnership may be limited to drinking at the same club.

Here is a list of words and phrases that indicate a person has skipped over something in his statement.

"After"
"Later on"
"Afterwards"
"Shortly thereafter"
"A short time later"
"A few minutes later"
"The next thing I know"
"The next thing I remember"

If you want to detect deception, listen for these words and phrases that span time. When a deceptive person gets to a point in his statement where he wants to withhold information, he will often quicken the pace of his story. He may use certain words or phrases that allow him to skip over something. Therefore, a good listener should identify this type of language. Back the person up in his statement and ask him to repeat what he did during the time frame he skipped over. If you feel he is still withholding information, ask specific questions about what he was doing during this point in his story.

CHAPTER 13

Articles

There are three articles in the English language: *a*, *an*, and *the*. These articles are classified as indefinite and definite. The articles *a* and *an* are the indefinite articles. They are used when you are talking about something that is not known to the person you are conversing with. For example, let's say your family just acquired a dog. In telling a friend about your new pet, you might say, "Yesterday, we bought a dog." The rules of grammar require you to use the indefinite article *a* because the person you are talking to does not know you purchased a dog.

The article *the* is a definite article. You use this article when the listener knows what you are talking about. For example, "The moon is bright tonight." We always refer to it as "the moon" and not "a moon" because there is only one moon. It is expected the listener knows which moon we are referring to. The same thing applies to the statement, "Give this note to the police department." Although there are many police departments it is understood the note needs to be given to a law enforcement agency. Therefore, even though this is the first time the word *police* is mentioned in the statement, the use of the article *the* is acceptable. We also use the article *the* when we have already introduced the person or thing we are talking about. Consider the following statement from a man who said he was robbed at gun point.

> "A man approached me from behind and told me that he had a gun. I could feel the gun in my back. He told me to give him my money which I did."

In the first sentence, the victim refers to the man and gun as "a man" and "a gun." This is a correct use of the article *a* because the victim is introducing the man and the gun to us. This is the first time we have heard about this man and his gun. In the second sentence, the victim changes his language and calls it "the gun." This too is the correct use of the article *the* because he has already told us about the gun. Think of it this way; you use the definite article *the* when you definitely know the listener understands what you are talking about.

When a person is being deceptive he will sometimes misuse these articles. He will violate the rules of grammar by introducing someone or something using the article *the* and not the articles *a* or *an*. Let's look at a statement given by a man who said he was robbed at an ATM machine.

> "I was walking away from an ATM machine when a man asked me if I knew what time it was. I told him that I did not have a watch. He then pulled out the gun and told me to go back to the machine. We walked back to the machine and he made me withdraw $200 from my account."

In the first two sentences, the subject correctly introduces the ATM machine, the man and the watch using the indefinite articles *a* and *an*. A problem arises in the third sentence when he introduces the gun. He refers to it as "the gun" and not "a gun." This means he either recognizes the gun or he is making up the story which happened to be the case. Because he is telling a lie he is not drawing his story from memory. He knows he is going to say the man had a gun. Therefore, he visualizes the man threatening him with a gun. In his mind, he has already introduced the gun. Therefore, he unknowingly uses the wrong article. We see further deception in this statement with the use of the pronoun *we*. The victim is telling us that he became partners with the robber. No victim of a robbery is going to partner-up with the thief.

We see another example of using the wrong article in an alleged kidnapping.

"I was standing at a bus stop when the van pulled up. A man jumped out of the van and told me to get in."

In the first sentence, the writer introduces the van to us using the article *the* and not the article *a*. By using the article *the*, the writer may be telling us he recognizes the van. Since this it is not the first time he has seen the van, he naturally uses the article *the* when describing it. Perhaps he willingly got into the van and now wants to say he was kidnapped. Another explanation for using the article *the* is that the writer is making up the story about being kidnapped. Since he is not telling the story as if he is reliving it, he mistakenly uses the wrong article.

In chapter eight, we looked at the statement from a woman who said that her husband accidentally shot himself. We saw she was being deceptive because she used passive language when she stated the gun "immediately went off." We see further signs of deception when we examine the articles in her statement. At the beginning of her statement, she said her husband "got a pistol" because he was going for a walk and he was "taking the pistol for protection." She correctly introduces the firearm as "a pistol." Now that she has mentioned the pistol she appropriately changes her language to "the pistol" when she talks about it a second time. A problem occurs the third time she refers to the pistol. In the statement we looked at earlier, she said, "While talking I heard a pistol cocked." She goes back to calling it as "a pistol." This violates the rules of grammar. Since she has already introduced the pistol, she should continually refer to it as "the pistol" throughout the rest of her statement. Perhaps though, she did not violate the rules of grammar. If another pistol entered into her story, then she would be required to use the article *a*. But where did the other pistol come from? Based on an analysis of her statement, all indications were her husband did not shoot himself but she shot her husband. Maybe he did have a pistol that he was going to take with him on his walk. Maybe she too had a pistol and she used her pistol to shoot her husband.

In chapter two, I talked about the husband who claimed he accidentally let his car roll off a cliff with his wife still in the car. She died in the crash. We saw that the morning she died there were problems in their relationship because he used the unique word *with* to distance himself from his wife; "That on Saturday morning I was with my wife Cathy." Later in his story we find the following statement: "I knew if someone went over the cliff in the car they would die." He may have used the pronoun *someone* because he is distancing himself from his wife. He may have also used this pronoun because he is not specifically talking about his wife. He is trying to talk in general terms. If someone went over a cliff, they are going to die. The laws of gravity pretty much tell us that. The problem is he did not refer to it as "a cliff" or "a car." If he was giving us an example that had a universal truth, he would have used the article *a* since he was introducing into his story an unknown cliff and an unknown car. By referring to it as "the cliff" and "the car" he was unknowingly telling us he was talking about the cliff his wife went over and the car she was in. He knew that if she went over this particular cliff in their car she would die. That is called premeditation!

Remember, the definite article *the* means the person definitely recognizes something. Consider the statement, "I heard a noise so I grabbed the shotgun and went outside." It would have been better if the writer showed possession and called it "my shotgun." There is a reason why he used the article *the* and not the pronoun *my*. However, the use of the article *the* does not necessarily mean he is being deceptive. He may have used the article *the* because this is the only shotgun he possesses. Likewise, if a person said, "I left the club at 10:00 p.m." his use of the article *the* indicates he may be making up the story or he is familiar with the club. He did not mention the name of the club which is something we would inquire about.

If you want to detect deception, pay close attention to the articles used by the subject. If the story is coming from memory, the person will tell it as if he is reliving it. This will cause him to properly introduce someone or something with the articles *a* and *an*. Once the introduction is made, he will then use the article *the*. If the subject uses the wrong articles, this is an indication of deception. It could be the subject recognizes the person or thing. It could also be the subject is fabricating the story and this caused him to use an incorrect article.

CHAPTER 14

Time References

Some statements will include time references. People may give a chronological listing of what they were doing and what time they did it. Other people may only mention a few time references such as what time they left or arrived at a location or what time an activity occurred. These time references commit the person to being at a certain place or performing a certain act at a specific time. Time references can sometimes show if the person is withholding information and/or being deceptive.

Omission is the most common form of deception. When giving a statement people will edit their statement. No one is going to state absolutely everything he knows or everything he did. Even a truthful person will only provide what information he thinks is important. As I mentioned earlier, deceptive people will usually give a truthful statement but they will leave out information they do not want to share. Some of this information may be incriminating. One way a deceptive person will withhold information is by quickening the pace of his story. This can be detected by examining the time references. A deceptive story may have some missing time. If the subject told you that he did something at 6:00 p.m. and then his next time reference is 9:00 p.m., you have a time gap of three hours. What was the subject doing from 6:00 p.m. to 9:00 p.m.? Consider the following answer to the question, "What did you do from the time you woke up to the time you went to sleep?"

> "I woke up at 8:30 and took a shower. I got dressed and read the newspaper. At 9:30, I drove to McDonalds on Arlington and ate a quick breakfast. After breakfast, I went to the Bradford Creek Golf Course and hit a bucket of balls. I left the golf course around 11:30 and drove to Wilson. At around 12:30, I met Craig Gottfried at Bills Barbecue and we had lunch together. I left Bills Barbecue around 1:30 and went home. Around 5:00 I worked in the yard cutting the grass. At 7:00, I made something to eat and got online and chatted with a friend in Ohio. We talked for about an hour. I got off the computer around 8:00 and then watched television. Around 10:00, my girlfriend Theresa called. I talked to her for about 30 minutes and then went to bed around 11:00."

As we examine the time references we see there is a large time gap between 1:30 and 5:00. The only information the subject provided during these three and one half hours was, "and went home around." Earlier he said that he left at 11:30 and arrived in Wilson at 12:30. We can surmise it takes about an hour to get to Wilson. If he left Bills Barbecue at 1:30 and went home, he should have arrived at his residence around 2:30. Stating next that he cut the grass at 5:00 is a clear sign he has withheld information about what he did from 1:30 to 5:00.

A more accurate way of analyzing the time references is to compare the objective time (any time of day mentioned by the subject) to the subjective time (the pace at which the subject writes his statement). The more hours there are per line the quicker the pace of the story. In the statement we just looked at, we find the following breakdown of the time references.

8:30 - 9:30	=	1 line for 1 hour	(1 hour per line)
9:30 - 11:30	=	2 lines for 2 hours	(1 hour per line)
11:30 - 12:30	=	.5 lines for 1 hour	(2 hours per line)
12:30 - 1:30	=	1 line for 1 hour	(1 hour per line)
1:30 - 5:00	=	.25 lines for 3.5 hours	(14 hours per line)
5:00 – 7:00	=	.75 lines for 2 hours	(2.6 hours per line)
7:00 – 8:00	=	1.5 lines for 1 hour	(.66 lines per hour)
8:00 – 10:00	=	.5 lines for 2 hours	(4 lines per hour)
10:00 – 11:00	=	1.25 lines for 1 hour	(.8 lines per hour)

By dividing the number of hours by the number of lines, you can determine the average number of hours per line (2 hours divided by 2 lines = 1 hour per line). In this case, you can see that from 1:30 to 5:00 the subject did not provide much information as to what he was doing. This time period averages 14 hours per line. It would be difficult for him to state in one line everything he did in a 14 hour time period.

In chapter twelve, we looked at a portion of a statement from a security guard who claimed he discovered money was missing from the company safe. Let's look at some more of his statement.

"I began to suspect that something was wrong about 3:00 a.m. when I noticed the back gate was unlocked. A few minutes later, I was convinced that something was wrong when I found the payroll office door unlocked and the safe opened. I recalled reading a story last year about money being taken from another facility. The guy who took the money wasn't caught. My first reaction was to call the boss. The boss has instructed us to call him in any emergency. He was pretty upset when I woke him up at 4:00 a.m."

We saw the security guard had skipped over something in his story when he used the phrase *a few minutes later*. We also see there is some missing time from 3:00 a.m. to 4:00 a.m. At 3:00 a.m., he noticed the back gate was unlocked. Only a few minutes later he finds the safe is open. After finding the safe open, he does not tell us what he was doing. He only mentions he was thinking about another robbery and that he should call his boss. Finally, at 4:00 a.m. he tells us he did call his boss. He discovered the money was missing around 3:00 a.m. but it takes him an hour to notify his boss. Obviously, there were other things going on during this hour that he has withheld. Since he would later admit that he took the money along with some other guards, most likely this is when they were emptying the safe.

Also notice that he said his "first reaction was to call the boss." This means he had to have had a second reaction. In his complete statement, he never mentions what his second reaction was. He refers to his boss as "the boss" and not "my boss." This means he is distancing himself from his boss. He never introduces his boss by name which is another sign he does not get along with his boss. Lastly, he uses the pronoun *us* which indicates there were other people with him that night even though he was the only security guard working that shift.

When a deceptive person mentions time references, he may state a time reference that is out of place. As he is making up his story may miscalculate his time. We see this in a statement given by a boyfriend concerning his girlfriend who was found murdered in her house. In his written affidavit, he mentions several time references.

> "The first time I called her was around 10:00 pm and she did not answer the phone. I then called her at 11:00 pm and at 12:00 am. At 12:15 am I went to her house. I knocked on the back door and blew my horn. I then went to the front and blew the horn again. I left Susan's house and went to Billy Adam's, house. I called Susan's mother from Billy's around 1:30 am to ask if she had any keys for Susan's house. I wanted to get in the house to check on her. I then called Susan again around 1:00 am, 2:00 am, 3:00 am and the last time was at 4:00 am."

Towards the end of his statement, the boyfriend states he called Susan's mother "around 1:30 am." Then he states he called Susan again "around 1:00 am." The subject is off on his time references. After calling Susan's mother at 1:30 a.m., he backs up in time to 1:00 a.m. and calls Susan. This would be an indication he is not speaking from memory but is making up the story.

When time references are mentioned in a deceptive statement they may not add up. It may not be possible for the subject to have done what he said he did in the amount of time he said he did it in. A subject may state he left his house at 7:00 p.m. and arrived at a friend's house at 7:30 p.m. If it actually takes 45 minutes to get to his friend's house then he may be lying. He may not have gone to his friend's house but did something else that he does not want to mention. If it only takes 10 minutes to get to his friend's house, then there is some time that is unaccounted for. What was he doing the other 20 minutes? Let's look at a statement of a man who said that he was car jacked.

> "Last Friday at 7:15 p.m., I left my house and got into my car. I was hungry so I decided to go out and get something to eat. My plan was to eat at Burger King on Memorial Drive. While driving to Burger King, I stopped at the light at the intersection of Memorial Drive and 10th street. It was now 7:30 p.m. and fairly dark outside. I was listening to some music in my car waiting for the light to turn green. All of the sudden my door opened and a man pointed a gun at me. He grabbed me and told me to get out the car which I did. He then jumped into my car and drove away. I ran to the gas station on the corner of Memorial Drive and 10th street. I told the person working there to call the police because my car had been stolen. Approximately five minutes later the police arrived at the gas station. I gave them a description of my car and of the thief."

In his statement, the victim only mentions two time references. He stated he left his house at 7:15 p.m. His car was stolen at the intersection of Memorial Drive and Tenth Street at 7:30 p.m. We would want to see how long it takes to drive from his house to the intersection of Memorial Drive and Tenth Street. If it only takes five minutes, then we need to find out what he was doing during the other ten minutes. If it takes longer to get to this intersection, then we have to wonder how he could have gotten there so quickly. If the time references do not add up, something is going on. Either he did something else that he hasn't told you or he is making up the story.

If you want to detect deception, pay attention to time references. Time references commit the subject to his statement. One way to see if the person has omitted telling you something is to look for a break in time. Missing time means you have missing information. If you have an out of place time reference or the time references do not add up, this indicates the story is not coming from memory. As the person is making up the story he forgets what time references he has already mentioned or he miscalculates certain time periods.

CHAPTER 15

Did the Subject Answer the Specific Question?

When asked a question most people will give an answer. However, if by answering the specific question the person will be embarrassed or will incriminate himself or someone else, he may choose to not answer the specific question. When a person does not answer a question he is withholding information. There are three ways that a person can avoid answering a question.

First, a person may refuse to say anything in response to a question. This is an obvious sign he probably has information that he does not want to share. He may not know the exact answer to the question but his silence tells you he is withholding some information.

Secondly, a person may state he is not going to answer the question. This too is an obvious signal he is concealing information. However, this type of person may offer an explanation as to why he is not going to answer the question. He is hoping that his explanation will satisfy the interviewer. We saw this with Al Gore during his 1988 campaign to be President. While on the campaign trail candidate Gore was asked if he ever smoked marijuana. He responded with the following answer.

> "I don't think it's an appropriate question. If you're asking me have I done that as an adult in my career; the answer is no. Have I done that within the last 15 years; the answer is no. Have I done anything beyond that; the answer is no. Did I experiment in college as a college student; my answer is that's an inappropriate question."[1]

Gore is telling the interviewer that he is not going to answer the question because it is an "inappropriate question." He will admit that in the last fifteen years as a career adult he has not smoked marijuana. However, he avoids answering the specific question if he ever smoked marijuana. Because he would not address his marijuana use in college, we can presume that he probably did smoke a joint while in school. This was confirmed several months later when finally he admitted that he did experiment in college.

George W. Bush did something similar when he ran for governor of Texas in 1994. While he was campaigning he was asked if ever used illegal drugs. He responded with the following answer.

> "Maybe I did. Maybe I didn't. What's the relevance? How I behaved as an irresponsible youth is irrelevant to this campaign."[2]

Bush deflects answering the question as to whether he used illegal drugs by stating that his actions as a youth are irrelevant to him wanting to be the governor of Texas. On January 17, 1995, he became the 46th governor of Texas.

A person better skilled at being deceptive will avoid answering a question using a third technique. He will give an answer that appears to answer the question but upon close examination we find he did not answer the specific question. Let's continue with examples of political candidates using unlawful substances. In chapter two, we looked at Bill Clinton's answer to his possible drug usage. While campaigning for the Presidency, Governor Clinton was asked, "Have you ever used illegal drugs?" He responded by saying, "I've never broken the laws of my country."[3] We saw that his use of the unique word *never* was appropriate because he was asked "Have you ever?" However, when we look at his answer we see that he did not answer the specific question. He was not asked if he had ever broken the laws of his country. He was asked if he had ever used illegal drugs. He gave an answer that sounded like he was answering the specific question but in reality he was avoiding answering the question. As I mentioned earlier, candidate Clinton eventually admitted that while attending college in England he experimented with marijuana.

Several years ago a gentleman who attended one of my seminars shared with me the story of how his wife wanted to have some friends over for dinner. His wife asked him to call their friends and invite them over. Several days later she asked her husband if he had made the phone call. He had completely forgotten about it so he told his wife "No. I haven't called them." Several more days went by and his wife asked him again if he had called their friends. Again, he had forgotten about it. However, this time he did not want to admit to his wife that he failed to remember to make the telephone call. On the other hand, he did not want to lie to his wife. So, he cleverly answered her question by stating, "I have not been able to get a hold of them." He gave his wife a truthful answer. He wasn't able to get a hold of their friends. Of course, the reason he could not get a hold of them is because he did not try to get a hold of them. He answered his wife's question but he did not answer her specific question, "Did you call them?"

In September 2007, Iranian President Mahmoud Ahmadinejad was in the United States to address the United Nations General Assembly. Prior to speaking at the United Nations, he spoke at Columbia University in New York. During his speech he was asked questions that were submitted by the students and faculty. The first question dealt with Israel.

Question: "Do you or your government seek the destruction of the state of Israel as a Jewish state?"

Ahmadinejad: "We love all nations. We are friends with the Jewish people. There are many Jews in Iran living peacefully with security. You must understand that in our constitution, in our laws, in the parliamentary elections, for every 150,000 people we get one representative in the parliament. For the Jewish community, one-fifth of this number they still get one independent representative in the parliament. So our proposal to the Palestinian plight is a humanitarian and democratic proposal. What we say is that to solve the 60-year problem we must allow the Palestinian people to decide about its future for itself. This is compatible with the spirit of the Charter of the United Nations and the fundamental principles enshrined in it. We must allow Jewish Palestinians, Muslim Palestinians and Christian Palestinians to determine their own fate themselves through a free referendum. Whatever they choose as a nation everybody should accept and respect. Nobody should interfere in the affairs of the Palestinian nation. Nobody should sow the seeds of discord. Nobody should spend tens of billions of dollars equipping and arming one group there. We say allow the Palestinian nation to decide its own future, to have the right to self-determination for itself. This is what we are saying as the Iranian nation."

(Applause)

Question: "Mr. President, I think many members of our audience would be - would like to hear a clearer answer to that question, that is – (interrupted by cheers and applause). Do you or your government seek the destruction of the state of Israel as a Jewish state? And I think you could answer that question with a single word, either yes or no."

Ahmadinejad: "And then you want the answer the way you want to hear it. Well, this isn't really a free flow of information. I'm just telling you where I - what my position is. (Applause) I'm asking you, is the Palestinian issue not an international issue of prominence or not? Please tell me, yes or no. (Laughter and applause) There's a plight of a people."[4]

We can clearly see that President Ahmadinejad did not answer the question if he wanted to see the destruction of Israel as a Jewish state. The moderator recognized this and asked the Iranian President this question again. On the second go around, the moderator added that he believed the President could answer the question with a *yes* or *no*. Still, President Ahmadinejad refused to answer the specific question. This would lead us to believe he does want to see Israel destroyed. This coincides with a statement he made at an anti-Israel demonstration in Tehran on October 26, 2005. He told a group of 4,000 students attending the rally that Israel must be "wiped off the map."[5] Sometimes people do not want to answer a question with a simple *yes* or *no*. They want to expound and explain themselves. That is fine but they still have to answer the specific question. If the question requires a *yes* or *no* answer, then somewhere in their lengthy answer we need to see a *yes* or *no*.

We see another example of giving an answer but not answering the specific question with Congressman Gary Condit. In 2001, Chandra Levy worked as an intern at the Federal Bureau of Prisons in Washington, D.C. On May 1 of that year, she disappeared from her apartment located in N.W. Washington, D.C. The police searched her apartment but found no signs of foul play. As the investigation into her disappearance continued, Chandra's father told the police his daughter was having an affair with Congressman Condit. The police questioned Condit and determined that he was not a suspect. However, many people felt that Condit was withholding information about Chandra's disappearance. This prompted Condit to appear on the ABC News program *Primetime Thursday*. Condit was interviewed by Connie Chung who began the interview with the following six straight forward questions.

Chung:	"Congressman Condit, do you know what happened to Chandra Levy?"
Condit:	"No, I do not."
Chung:	"Did you have anything to do with her disappearance?"
Condit:	"No, I didn't."
Chung:	"Did you say anything or do anything that could have caused her to drop out of sight?"
Condit:	"You know, Chandra and I never had a cross word."
Chung:	"Do you have any idea if there was anyone who wanted to harm her?"
Condit:	"No."
Chung:	"Did you cause anyone to harm her?"
Condit:	"No."
Chung:	"Did you kill Chandra Levy?"
Condit:	"I did not."[6]

Condit directly answers five of the six questions with "No" or "I did not." However, there is one question he gives an answer but he does not answer the specific question.

Chung: "Did you say anything or do anything that could have caused her to drop out of sight?"

Condit: "You know, Chandra and I never had a cross word."

Condit was not asked, "Did you have a cross word with Chandra Levy?" He was asked if he said or did anything that could have caused her to drop out of sight. By not answering the specific question, he is withholding information. Many people believe that Condit and Levy did have an affair. Chandra's aunt said that Chandra told her about the affair. If this is true, we see why Condit did not answer this question. All relationships have their ups and downs. Since he did not kill her and he did not know what happened to her, he may have been thinking to himself that perhaps he did say something that caused her to drop out of sight. Therefore, instead of answering the question with, "No, I did not say or do anything" he chose not to answer the specific question and passed it off by saying, "Chandra and I never had a cross word." He clearly was using the unique word *never* as a substitute for the word *no*.

On May 22, 2002, Chandra Levy's remains were found in Washington's Rock Creek Park. On May 28, 2002, the medical examiner for the District of Columbia declared her death as a homicide. On March 3, 2009, an arrest warrant was issued for Ingmar Guandique charging him with Chandra's death. In July 2001, Guandique had been arrested for assaulting a woman in the same park. On May 27, 2009, Guandique pled not guilty to the charges that he killed Chandra Levy. He was convicted of her murder in November 2010 and in February 2011 he was sentenced to sixty years in prison.

In chapter one, we looked at a portion of Roger Clemens's testimony before Congress concerning steroid use in major league baseball. Congress was investigating Brian McNamee's claim that he injected Clemens with performance enhancing drugs. During his testimony we find the following exchange between Clemens and Representative John Mica.

Mica: "You don't think he (Brian McNamee) is telling the truth then?"

Clemens: "Brian McNamee has never given me growth hormone or steroids."[7]

Clemens gives an answer but he does not answer the specific question. By the way Mica phrased the question he was simply looking for Clemens to confirm that McNamee was not telling the truth. This is the perfect opportunity for Clemens to state, "That is correct. He is not telling the truth." Instead of calling McNamee a liar, which is what Clemens wants Congress to believe, he avoids answering the question concerning whether or not McNamee is telling the truth. This would lead one to believe that Brian McNamee is not lying when he says he injected Roger Clemens with steroids.

On the morning of April 19, 1995, a truck parked in front of the Alfred P. Murrah federal building in Oklahoma City, Oklahoma exploded killing one hundred sixty-eight people. At the time, it was the worst case of terrorism on U.S. soil. Timothy McVeigh was soon taken into custody and charged with the bombing. McVeigh was keeping quiet but after spending two months in jail he decided to tell his side of the story. Along with his attorney Stephen Jones, he granted an interview with two columnists from *Newsweek* magazine. After asking him some preliminary questions, they then asked him the big question.

> Newsweek: "This is the question that everybody wants to know. Did you do it?"
> McVeigh: "The only way we can really answer that is that we are going to plead not guilty."
> Jones: "And we're going to go to trial."
> Newsweek: "But you've got a chance right now to say, 'Hell no!'"
> Jones: "Well, but that –"
> McVeigh: "We can't do that."[8]

McVeigh was asked, "Did you do it?" While he gives an answer he does not answer the specific question. He does not answer with a *yes* or *no*. This means he is withholding some information. Saying he is going to plead not guilty is not the same thing as saying he did not do it. The interviewers even point this out by telling him he has the chance right now to deny involvement in this crime. McVeigh responds by saying, "We can't do that." The reason McVeigh "can't do that" is because he knows he set the bomb off and he does not want to lie about it.

In addition to not answering the question, we also find some interesting information when we look at the language McVeigh used. He states, "The only way we can really answer that." Although he was asked if he did it, McVeigh uses the pronoun *we* instead of *I*. Perhaps he is referring to a co-conspirator. Terry Nichols would eventually be convicted of conspiring with McVeigh in the bombing. Most likely the *we* refers to his attorney who was with him during the interview. They have decided to plead not guilty. However, the question was directed towards McVeigh. McVeigh chose not to personalize his answer by using the pronoun *we*.

We also see that McVeigh used the word *really* in his answer. The word *really* means "truly" or "genuinely." McVeigh is saying the only way they can truthfully answer this question is to state, "we are going to plead not guilty." Why is this the only way they can answer this question? Because, if he said, "No, I didn't do it" that would be a lie. Since he does not want to lie, he chooses not to answer the specific question.

McVeigh would use this same tactic nine months later when he was interviewed by *TIME* magazine correspondent Patrick E. Cole.

Cole: "Have you ever built a bomb?"

McVeigh: "I've never had my hand on one. I used to watch other people do it. I won't go into that. There were plastic soda bottles. They would put vinegar and baking soda in and screw the cap on and it would burst."[9]

McVeigh gives what appears to be a good answer, "I've never had my hand on one." If he has never touched a bomb, then it would be difficult for him to have built a bomb. However, the question requires a *yes* or *no* answer. McVeigh chooses not to answer the specific question which means he is withholding some information. The reason McVeigh did not answer this question with a *no* is because he does not want to tell a direct lie. Therefore, he denies building a bomb by saying he has never had his hand on one. Although this too is most likely a lie it is easier for him to lie by using the unique word *never* than it is to say, "No, I have never built a bomb."

Remember, everyone has their own personal dictionary. Everyone has their own definition for the word *bomb*. When McVeigh talks about a bomb he refers to putting vinegar and baking soda into plastic bottles. This combustible mixture is something most kids experiment with. They even make toy submarines that can be placed in a pool that are propelled by these ingredients. It could be that McVeigh views a bomb as being a plastic bottle that contains this concoction. If that is true, then in his mind he may be giving a truthful answer when he says he has never touched a bomb. He may have handled hand grenades and other explosives while in the military. He may have helped build that explosive truck which contained barrels of ammonia nitrate and fuel oil. However, he has never had his hand on a bomb.

On August 10, 1995, a federal grand jury indicted McVeigh for using of a weapon of mass destruction. He was also charged with eight counts of first-degree murder for the deaths of eight federal officers who were killed in the explosion. On June 2, 1997, he was found guilty on all counts. Ten days later the jury recommended that he receive the death penalty. On June 11, 2001, Timothy McVeigh was executed by lethal injection at the U.S. Penitentiary in Terre Haute, Indiana.

In chapter six, I talked about cyclist Floyd Landis who won the 2006 Tour de France but was stripped of his victory after he tested positive for a banned performance enhancing drug. We saw that at his 2006 news conference Landis used present tense language in his denial which indicated he was not denying that he ever took an illegal substance. During this news conference a reporter asked him about lying to his mother.

> Reporter: "We were over with your mom today in Farmersville and she said that you called her and said that you had done nothing wrong, so a very pointed, forward question here. Would you ever lie to your mom?"
>
> Landis: "You've met my mom. I don't think anyone has lied to my mom."[10]

Although Landis gives an answer he does not answer the specific question, "Would you lie to your mom?" By stating he does not think "anyone" has lied to his mom, Landis is trying to include himself in that group of "anyone." He is hoping everyone will assume he has not lied to his mother. However, we do not assume but we only believe what people tell us. Landis has not told us that he did not lie to his mother. Since he did not answer the specific question, he is withholding information. Now that he has admitted to doping, we can see why he did not answer this question.

On May 21, 2011, a sexually suggestive photo was sent to a 21-year-old female college student through U.S. Congressman Anthony Weiner's Twitter account. Weiner denied he sent the photo stating that his Twitter account had been hacked. On June 1, 2011, Weiner was interviewed by CNN's Wolf Blitzer about the photo controversy.

> Blitzer: "This is the picture. I'm sure you've seen it by now. Is this you?"

Weiner: "I can tell you this. We have a firm that we've hired – I've seen it, it's – I've seen it – a firm that we've hire to get to the bottom of it. I can tell you this, that photos can be manipulated. Photos can be one thing changed to look like something else. We're going to try to get to the bottom of what happened…"[11]

Weiner goes on giving a lengthy answer but no where in his answer does he answer Blitzer's specific question. He never tells Blitzer, "No. That is not me in the picture." This means he was withholding some information. Several days after this interview, Weiner admitted to sending the racy picture.

If you want to detect deception, look to see if the person has answered the specific question. A truthful person will answer specific questions with direct answers. A deceptive person will avoid answering the question. He will give an answer which may sound like he has answered the question but the reality is he has not answered the specific question. Not answering the specific question means the person is withholding information. You should ask the question a second time and attempt to force him to give you a direct answer.

CHAPTER 16

Did the Subject Answer the Question with a Question?

When a person answers a question with a question, it means he was asked a sensitive question. There can be a variety of reasons why a subject finds the topic so touchy. It could be he is guilty of something or he has additional information he does not want to share. Therefore, he will redirect the conversation by answering the question with a question. For example, if the question asked was, "Did you take the money?" some deceptive answers might be, "You think I did?" "Are you accusing me of stealing?" "Don't you know me better than that?"

By answering with a question, the subject is looking for a response from the interviewer. He is hoping this will allow him to avoid answering the specific question. In some cases, the person may not have anything to hide but yet he finds the question to be displeasing. For example, a husband may ask his wife, "Do you want to go bowling Wednesday night?" She may respond, "Isn't the church having their cantata Wednesday night?" This is her way of politely saying they are not going bowling but will be at church. Even though she is not being deceptive, the fact she answered her husband's question with a question means she was asked a sensitive question. She does not want to miss the cantata as her husband is suggesting.

Most of the time when a person uses this tactic he will answer the question with a question, but he will then follow it up by answering the specific question.

Question: "Did you take the money?"
Answer: "Did I take the money? No."

The subject answered with a question but he was not waiting for the interviewer to respond to his question. After answering with a question, he then gave a direct denial. In this situation, the person answered with a question because the question was sensitive and he is stalling for time to think about how he should answer the question. He cannot give a straight answer without first pondering his answer. In regards to the missing money, the subject repeated the question, "Did I take the money?" This is a classic way of stalling for time. He is giving the appearance he is making sure he heard the question correctly. However, in most cases he is simply buying himself some time to think about how he should answer the question. The person may be thinking he knows money is missing and he knows who took it. However, he was asked if he took the money which he did not do. Therefore, this leads him to finish his answer with a truthful "no." Even though he answered the question truthfully, since he first answered it with a question this tells us he was asked a sensitive question and he probably has additional information.

When I worked at the U.S. Marshals Service Training Academy we had staff sweatshirts that identified us as being an instructor. One day I walked into our building and placed my sweatshirt on the counter by the receptionist. I then went around the corner to check my mail box. When I returned to the counter my sweatshirt was no longer there. I then asked the receptionist, "Did you take my sweatshirt?" She responded, "Did I take it? No." She answered my question with a question. She wasn't waiting for me to answer her question because she quickly responded with "no" which told me she was probably being truthful. However, she couldn't just say "no." She first had to answer with a question because she wanted some time to think about her answer. It wasn't too hard to figure out what was going on. She saw the person who took my sweatshirt and she wasn't sure if she should give that person up. People's words will betray them. Answering a question with a question is one way people will let us know they have additional information.

In 2004, Senator John Kerry ran for President against incumbent President George W. Bush. A group known as the Swift Vote Veterans for Truth opposed Kerry's candidacy. Kerry had served in Vietnam as a commander of a swift boat. The group challenged Kerry's military record with a series of television ads. This helped to create the term *swiftboating* which many people regard as an unfair political smear campaign. In September of 2004, a reporter with *Time* magazine asked First Lady Laura Bush about these ads.

Reporter: "Do you think these swiftboat ads are unfair to John Kerry?"
First Lady: "Do I think they're unfair. Not really."[1]

The First Lady answered the specific question by saying "Not really." However, before she could give that answer she first answered the question with a question; "Do I think they're unfair?" Since she did not give the reporter time to answer her question, we know she did this to give herself some time to think about her answer. We should ask ourselves, "What is the First Lady thinking about?" We have a good idea of what was on her mind when we look at her answer of "Not really." The phrase *not really* does not mean *no*. The word *really* is a word that indicates untruthfulness. Which would you prefer to hear? "I love you" or "I love you, really." Adding the word "really" weakens the statement. This tells us the First Lady probably does think the switfboat ads were unfair. However, since her husband was running for re-election she did not want to say that. This caused her to answer the question with a question and to give a weak denial.

In chapters one and two, I talked about Casey Anthony and the disappearance of her daughter Caylee. We saw how Anthony used deceptive language when she said, "I don't have a clue" concerning the whereabouts of her daughter. She also used the unique word *actually* when telling the 911 operator she had spoken to Caylee on the phone. When we look again at her conversation with the 911 operator we see that Anthony answered a question with a question.

911:	"Hi. What can you - can you tell me what's going on a little bit?"
Anthony:	"I'm sorry?"
911:	"Can you tell me a little bit what's going on?"
Anthony:	"My daughter's been missing for the last thirty-one days."[2]

Anthony did not repeat the question which is what a lot of people will do. Instead, she asked the question, "I'm sorry?" and waited for the operator to answer her question. It is possible that Anthony did not hear the 911 operator's question. However, the far majority of the time when a person answers a question with any type of question it means he or she was asked a sensitive question.

In chapter four, we looked at a portion of Greta Van Susteren's interview with Joran Van der Sloot the prime suspect in Natalee Holloway's disappearance. When we look at more of her interview with Van der Sloot we see that Van der Sloot likes to answer questions with a question. Van der Sloot said he met Natalee and her friends at a casino. This prompted Van Susteren to ask the following question.

> Van Susteren: "Interested in any of them at the poker table?"
> Van der Sloot: "Interested? No, not really. I was more talking - the girl that was sitting next to me I was - I thought she was pretty and I was talking to her. And when I went – what the point was for going to Carlos 'n Charlie's was I wanted to actually meet up with her."[3]

When asked if he was interested in any of the girls at the poker tableVan der Sloot answers with the question "Interested?" He then uses the same language as First Lady Laura Bush, "not really." This tells us he was interested in someone at the poker table. Van der Sloot confirms this when he says, "I wanted to actually meet up with her."

As the interview continued we find the following questions and answers:

Van der Sloot:	"So, you get the phone call from your father. Were you at the table when you got the call?"
Van der Sloot:	"When I got the phone call? No, we were - I - we'd actually left already and when we were going to the car to go to another casino, and that's when we got that phone call."
Van Susteren:	"Where were you planning to go?"
Van der Sloot:	"We were planning to go to, in town, the Excelsior casino there. Or not the Excelsior the Crystal casino there."
Van Susteren:	"All right. So when you're standing at the car, did he say anything to you all? Did he ask you about the night before? Did he discuss the night before?"
Van der Sloot:	"No, he didn't, he didn't ask me anything."
Van Susteren:	"Never mentioned it at all?"
Van der Sloot:	"Never mentioned it at all."
Van Susteren:	"Do you find that unusual or not?"
Van der Sloot:	"No."
Van Susteren:	"It's just normal?"
Van der Sloot:	"Yes."
Van Susteren:	"Ok. So your father, so what did your father say in the phone call?"
Van der Sloot:	"In the phone call? Yes, he called me and said there's people here in front of the house looking for their daughter."[4]

In the first question, Van Susteren asked Van der Sloot about the phone call he received from his father. She asked him if he was at the table when he got the call. Van der Sloot responds with the question, "When I got the phone call?" This means the question about getting a phone call from his father is a sensitive question. Van der Sloot then answers the question but in doing so he changes his pronouns.

    Van der Sloot: "When I got the phone call? No, we were - I - we'd actually left already and when we were going to the car to go to another casino, and that's when we got that phone call."

He goes from "we were" to "I" to "we'd actually left already." Changing pronoun is an indication of deception. This may occur because he is making up the story and not relying on his memory. He goes on to say, "that's when we got that phone call." He was asked about the phone call that *he* received but he uses the plural pronoun *we* in talking about the phone call.

The next five questions Van der Sloot answered with a direct answer. In the last question, Van Susterern asked him again about the phone call his father made to him; "So what did your father say in the phone call?" Van der Sloot answers with the question, "In the phone call?" Twice when asked about the phone call he received from his father Van der Sloot stalled for time by answering the question with a question. Chances are his father told him more than just there are people in front of the house looking for their daughter.

Van Susteren ends the interview with the following questions:

Van Susteren:	"Other than the lie about the Holiday Inn and the two guards (inaudible) did you lie to the police at all?"
Van der Sloot:	"That's what I said to you about that, that Deepak Kalpoe and Satish dropped me off at my house. That's (inaudible)."
Van Susteren:	"So two lies essentially?"
Van der Sloot:	"Yes."
Van Susteren:	"Any other lies?"
Van der Sloot:	"Any other lies? No."
Van Susteren:	"Know anything else about this?"
Van der Sloot:	"No."
Van Susteren:	"Nothing about what happened to Natalee?"
Van der Sloot:	"No."[5]

It appears Van der Sloot did not answer the first question, "Did you lie to the police at all?" He gave an answer but he did not answer the specific question unless it is in the inaudible part of his answer. If he did not answer the specific question, he is withholding information about lying to the police.

He answered the second question but that was easy for him to do. Van Susteren did not ask him, "Did you only tell two lies?" Instead, she used the word *essentially*. What Van der Sloot is saying in his answer is, "Yes, I essentially only told two lies." That leaves the possibility he told other lies.

Van Susteren then narrowed it down and asked him, "Any other lies?" Van der Sloot answered her question by repeating the question. He has to think about if he told any other lies. This would lead us to believe that perhaps there are some other lies he has failed to mention.

In April 2011, golfer Tiger Woods injured his left knee and Achilles tendon while competing in the Masters Tournament. In order to give his body time to heal, Woods chose not to participate in the U.S. Open which was held in June of the same year. With Woods not competing in the tournament, his long time caddie Steve Williams was given an opportunity to temporarily caddie for golfer Adam Scott. The following month Woods announced he would miss the British Open due to his injured left leg. This allowed Williams to again caddie for Scott.

Speculation grew that perhaps the Woods/Williams partnership had dissolved. While caddying for Scott at the British Open, Williams was asked if he was still working for Woods. He responded, "Why would you ask a question like that?"[6] Williams answered the reporter's question with a question. This means he was asked a sensitive question. The reason Williams was on edge is because two weeks earlier he met with Woods who told him they would no longer be working together. Williams and Woods were keeping the split quiet so it would not be a distraction to Adam Scott during the British Open. Several days after the British Open ended Woods announced on his website that the Woods and Williams player-caddie relationship had ended.

As I have already mentioned, you can watch a television show and figure out who is lying by listening to what a person is saying. Even though they are actors and this may be a fictional show, the show's writers will have them answer a question just like a deceptive person would answer it. One day I was watching *Walker Texas Ranger* starring Chuck Norris. Walker and his partner were looking for Chico Gonzalez. They went to Gonzalez's last known place of employment and interviewed his boss in an effort to locate Gonzalez. This led to the following question and answer.

> Question: "Have you seen Chico Gonzalez?"
> Answer: "Chico Gonzalez? I can't say that I have."

The boss answered the question with a question. He did not wait for them to answer his question and clarify if indeed it was Chico Gonzalez they were looking for. This clearly tells us he used this tactic to buy himself some time so he could think about his answer. When we look at the rest of his answer we see that he said he "can't say" he has seen Gonzalez. This is different than saying, "I have not seen Chico Gonzalez." The reason the boss can't say he has seen Gonzalez is because he does not want to give him up. It is like he is saying, "I can't say where he is because you will arrest him." As soon as Walker and his partner left the business Chico Gonzalez appeared from a back room.

If you want to detect deception, listen to see if the person answers a question with a question. If he answers with any type of question, it means he was asked a sensitive question. You will want to find out why the question is so sensitive. The person may be thinking how big of a lie he should tell or how much information he should share. If he asks you, "Could you repeat the question?" you will have to decide if he did not hear the question or if he is stalling for time to think about his answer.

Part 2

The Language of a Liar

Written Statements

Written Statements

Written statements often provide more information than verbal statements. This is because a written statement may contain things that are not found in a verbal statement such as the person's writing style or crossed out words. The other reason written statements can be quite revealing is because you can take your time when analyzing the statement. You can read and examine the statement several times. Sometimes you will see things in the second or third reading that you did not see the first time reading the statement. Some techniques such as analyzing the subject's personal dictionary can be difficult to use when listening to a verbal statement. When the statement is preserved in writing, you can underline, circle, and highlight the language in an effort to see exactly what the subject is saying. When reading a written statement, you do not have to think about the next question you are going to ask the subject. Therefore, all of your concentration can be devoted to analyzing the written statement allowing you to obtain more information. I often receive written statements that are ten years old. The Statement Analysis techniques still work because the statement has been recorded. The subject cannot say he did not say something because we have the statement in his own handwriting. This also applies to statements written in an email or text messages. Even though the statement may not be written with a pen or pencil it is still the person's own words.

All of the techniques we have looked at in the first sixteen chapters in reference to a verbal statement can also be applied to a written statement. The language, verb tenses, and pronouns that one uses in a written statement can reveal a person's true thoughts. Let's take a look at some other things you should look for when analyzing a written statement.

CHAPTER 17

Crossed Out Words

Unlike verbal statements written statements may contain crossed out words. A person may cross out a word because he made a spelling mistake. Once he crosses out the word he writes it again correctly. This is usually insignificant. There are other times when a person crosses out a word or words not because he has a spelling error but because he is being deceptive. Without realizing it, the person starts to write the truth. He then recognizes he is about to give an incriminating statement. Therefore, he crosses out the incriminating part and continues on with his deceptive statement. It is this type of cross out that can betray a person's true thoughts.

I once investigated a case in which a maintenance man was accused of taking a student's wallet from a locker room. The student who reported the stolen wallet gave the following written statement:

"On May 12, 1998 at around 6:30 pm, I was in the locker room sitting at my locker. As I was getting dressed a man ~~ask~~ was standing by my locker when I had my back turned. When I turned around he seemed startled and asked for change for a dollar. I told him that I had no change. He then left. I then got dressed and went to my room. That is when I noticed my wallet was missing."

The alleged victim crossed out one word with a single line. Therefore, it is easy to see the word he had crossed out was the word *ask*. The student started to write the truth. As he was getting dressed the maintenance man asked him if he had change for a dollar. However, he saw this as an opportunity to blame the maintenance man for his missing wallet. So, he stopped writing and crossed out the word *ask*. He then set the stage for this crime. He wrote he had his back towards the maintenance man and when he turned around the maintenance man was startled. He then continued with the truthful story stating the maintenance man asked for change for a dollar and he told him he did not have any change.

When I interviewed the maintenance man he confirmed my suspicion. He stated that he wanted to get something out of the vending machine so he asked this student if he had change for a dollar. When the student said he had no change he then asked another student in the locker room who was able to change a dollar. It turned out the maintenance man did not steal the student's wallet. The student had lost his wallet earlier in the day.

The Springfield Three is a missing person case that occurred on June 7, 1992 in Springfield, Missouri. On June 6, 1992, Suzie Streeter and Stacy McCall graduated from Kickapoo High School. That night the two girls celebrated their accomplishment by attending several parties. When they were done partying, the girls spent the night at Suzie's house. Suzie lived with her mother Sherrill Levitt in central Springfield. Sherrill was a single mother who worked as a hair dresser.

The next morning Suzie and Stacy's friend Janelle Kriby called Suzie's house but no one answered. Janelle, Suzie and Stacy had planned to go to an amusement park that day. Around noon Janelle and her boyfriend Mike went to Suzie's house but they got no response when they knocked on the door. Janelle saw that the women's three cars were parked in the driveway so she thought they must be in the house. Janelle and Mike were able to crack open a door and enter the residence. They found no one in the house. There were no signs of a struggle or forced entry. A television was still on and the women's purses had been left behind. Almost two decades later the three women are still missing.

Over the years the Springfield Police have followed numerous leads and interviewed several suspects in trying to solve this case. One of the prime suspects is Robert Craig Cox. In 1985, Cox pled guilty to attempting to kidnap two young women in California. He received a nine-year prison sentence. While serving his sentence in California he was extradited to Orange County, Florida where he was convicted of murdering a 19-year-old girl in 1978. However, the Florida Supreme Court reversed Cox's conviction stating that the evidence created only a suspicion of guilt. Cox was then sent back to California to finish out his sentence. When he was paroled, Cox returned home to Springfield, Missouri. During the time the three women disappeared, Cox was working as a utility locator in south-central Springfield. Although a suspect, Cox's girlfriend provided him with an alibi. She stated that Cox was with her in church the morning the women disappeared.

In 1995, Cox was arrested in Decatur, Texas for holding a gun on a 12-year-old girl during a robbery. He was convicted and sentenced to life in a Texas State Prison. The Springfield Police interviewed Cox in prison about the missing women. Cox teased the investigators by implying he knew the women were dead and where they were buried. Cox's ex-girlfriend then recanted her story that Cox was with her in church the day the women disappeared. She testified before a grand jury that Cox asked her to lie for him. Despite this new information the police did not have enough evidence to indict Cox for the murder of the three women.

Throughout the years Cox has continued to reach out from his cell and hint that he was involved in the women's disappearance. In May 1997, Cox wrote a letter to the *Springfield News-Leader* a major newspaper in Springfield, Missouri. In his letter, Cox wrote about how the police wanted him to tell them where the bodies could be found.

> "Then Sgt. Routh told me how he had taken over the case. He told me he didn't think I was involved in this xxx case, then in his next words he wanted to bring closure to this case by telling him where the bodies were. I told them I wanted closure too. I'm tired of the harassment I have received because of my association to this case. Then I told Sgt. Routh if I told could tell him where the bodies were then he would come after me with an indictment and seek the death penalty."[1]

In the first paragraph, Cox heavily crosses out a word to the point that it is difficult to tell what he had first written. In the second paragraph, he crosses out a word that is somewhat readable. It appears he crossed out the word "told." If true, then the sentence he originally was going to write was, "Then I told Sgt. Routh if I told him where the bodies were…" Cox realizes this is an incriminating statement because he is admitting he knows where the women are buried. So, he changes his language and writes, "if I ~~told~~ could tell him were the bodies were…" In this statement, he is not admitting that he knows where the bodies are buried.

There is circumstantial evidence that Cox was involved in the disappearance of these women. In his own language, we see he may have admitted to being involved in this crime. However, he has never been charged with their deaths. The disappearance of the three women remains a mystery.

We find a crossed out word in the ransom note involving the murder of JonBenet Ramsey. The writer of the ransom note wrote that it may be possible for JonBenet to be returned to her parents sooner than later.

> "If we monitor you getting the money early, we might call you early to arrange an earlier delivery of the money and hence a [sic] earlier ~~delivery~~ pick-up of your daughter."[2]

What the writer was originally going to write is that if the Ramsey's delivered the money early the kidnappers would deliver JonBenet early. The writer then realized a kidnapper would not deliver the hostage. Instead, a kidnapper would tell the parents where their daughter could be found. This led the writer to cross out the word *delivery* and write the word *pick-up*. It is unlikely a true kidnapper would make this mistake. This crossed out word indicates this was not a kidnapping that turned into a murder. Instead, after JonBenet was killed, someone wrote a ransom note to make it look like this was an attempted kidnapping. However, in this part of the ransom note the writer forgot to think like a kidnapper. The Ramsey's have always insisted this was a kidnapping that went bad. However, this crossed out word indicates otherwise.

In chapter ten, I talked about how everyone has their own personal dictionary. One of the statements we looked at was from a woman who said that she was sexually assaulted after a night of partying. In her statement, we see that she crossed out a word.

> "I arrived at Carol's house around 10:00 p.m. for a party she was having. At round 4:00 a.m., I went to bed in the guest bedroom. At 5:00 a.m., I felt someone lying in bed with me. ~~They~~ He was touching and rubbing me. I moved away from him and he moved closer to me. I rolled over + he put his hand between my legs. When I realized what he was doing I pushed him away and got out of the bed. I then went to Carol's room and told her what happened."

It was easy to see in her handwritten statement she had crossed out the word *they*. She then replaced the word *they* with the word *he*. Remember that changing pronouns is an indication of deception. If she is making up the story, she is not drawing her entire story from memory. This causes her to use the wrong pronoun. It is also possible she first used the "singular they" pronoun because at that moment while she was lying in bed she did not know if the person was a man or a woman. However, as she is writing her story she knows it was a man so she decided to use the pronoun *he*. One crossed out word in a statement does not automatically mean the person is lying. It is just one more thing to consider as you analyze the entire statement.

When a person crosses out a word he will usually write something else. However, there are times when a person will cross out a word or words and will not add anything to it. A good example of this is a letter written by O.J. Simpson concerning the murder of his ex-wife Nicole Brown Simpson. On June 17, 1994, Simpson failed to turn himself into the Los Angeles Police Department. This self-surrender was worked out by his attorneys. On that same day, Simpson's friend, Robert Kardashian, read for the media a letter written by Simpson. The letter would become known as the "suicide letter" because in it Simpson says goodbye to many of his friends. The letter printed in the press and read on national television began, "To whom it may concern: First, everyone understand I had nothing to do with Nicole's murder."[3] The problem is that this is not what Simpson wrote. When you look at the letter you can see that he crossed out two words. Simpson's letter actually reads, "To whom it may concern: First, everyone understand I hxx nothing to do with Nicole's murder."[4] The second crossed out word is harder to read. Some believe he crossed out the words *I have* while others think he crossed out the words *I had*. Regardless of what he crossed out, the point is Simpson crossed out these two words but did not write something else to replace them. When a person crosses out a word he is telling us he does not want that word in his statement. He is in essence saying, "I don't want to say that." That is what Simpson did. He took himself out of his denial. The way his letter actually reads is as follows: "To whom it may concern: First, everyone understand nothing to do with Nicole's murder." Who had nothing to do with Nicole's murder? We do not know because in his denial there is no subject. Later in his letter, Simpson wrote, "Inside I had no ~~dxxxx~~ doubt that in the future we would be close as friend [sic] or more."[5] It appears Simpson misspelled the word *doubt* and rewrote the word. This is usually no big deal. Everyone makes mistakes. However, at the beginning of his letter his crossed out words were not a mistake. In his own letter, that he was freely writing, Simpson could not bring himself to state that he did not kill his ex-wife. When we look at the language he used we also see that Simpson used the weaker denial of stating that he had "nothing to do with" her death as opposed to saying, "I didn't kill her."

If you want to detect deception, closely examine crossed out words. See if you can determine why the person crossed out a portion of his statement. This may be information the writer does not want to share with you. It could also be the writer simply misspelled a word. Tell the writer that if he makes a mistake to draw a single line through it. You want to be able to read what the writer has crossed out. The subject may have written an incriminating statement and then changed it. Even if the writer has heavily crossed out a word so it cannot be read, you may be able to glean some information based on where in his statement the cross out occurs.

CHAPTER 18

Story Breakdown

Nearly every story is comprised of three segments: before, during, and after. This is especially true if the subject is writing about an incident he experienced. He will begin his story by writing what was happening before the incident took place. This is known as the "Before the Incident" segment. He will then describe the incident that took place. This is known as the "During the Incident" segment. He will finish his story telling us what happened after the incident ended. This is known as the "After the Incident" segment. By examining how much time a writer devotes towards each segment, you can determine if the subject gave a truthful statement.

Both truthful and deceptive stories will have a significant beginning. In a truthful story, there is always something going on before the incident occurred. The subject should state everything that happened leading up to the incident. If the subject is making up a story, then there was no incident. However, to make his story sound believable the writer will set the stage for his deception. He will mention things that were going on prior to the incident. The "Before the Incident" segment in a truthful story will consist of approximately 25% of the entire story. In a deceptive story, this portion will be about 35% of the entire story.

The "During the Incident" segment in a truthful and deceptive story will make up the majority of the statement. The subject will spend a great amount of time writing about what happened to him or what he witnessed. In both cases, this will be comprised of about 50% of the entire story.

The "After the Incident" segment is the portion of the story that usually lets you know if it is a truthful story. In a truthful statement, there is always something else going on once the incident has ended. The person may have experienced injuries, pain, or emotional feelings. Perhaps a phone call was made to 911 and the police responded. The subject may have filed a police report or had to go to the hospital. Other people may have been present when the incident occurred and provided help once it was over. Because other things are still happening, a truthful story will have a significant ending. The writer will tell us what was going on when the incident was over. This segment will make up about 25% of the story. Deceptive stories often have a very short ending. Since the incident never occurred, there was never an ending. Making up an ending is not important to a deceptive person. He only wants to talk about the incident and will forget to include the "After the Incident" segment or this segment will be very short comprised of only about 10% of the entire story.

Consider the following story about a vacation. I have broken down the three segments into three sections.

> "The one thing I had most often thought about in my adolescent years finally became a reality in the summer of 1985. Several of my friends and I had often spoke of taking a trip across country but lack of money and a dependable

vehicle always kept the dream out of reach. Finally in the summer of 1985, my friend Jay and I decided it was time to do what we had always dreamt of. We decided to pool our money together, service my vehicle and prepare it for the trip. I owned a 1979 Chevrolet Monte Carlo at the time and was apprehensive about taking it on such a long trip. We decided that we had made enough excuses not to take the trip and we were just going to do it."

"We left on May 28 and headed west from New Hampshire. We each had $1000.00 and decided on 2 to 3 weeks for our trip. I loved the adventure of the unknown and being in places that I had never been in before. The most exciting part of the trip was stopping in small towns and cities across the U.S. and talking with people. I loved watching the landscape change from state to state and came to realize how beautiful and how much of the country there is to see. I really wish that we had more money to spend on some of the more touristy things but we could not afford to see all the things we would have like to. We saved money by sleeping on the side of the road in rest areas and secluded areas. I'll never forget the beautiful city skylines and rolling hill and farmlands we passed. I started realizing that I was part of a bigger picture, much bigger than just my hometown. We decided not to spend much time in big cities but rather visit small towns and talked to small town people because we felt it would be safer and they friendlier. As we neared the West Coast and got closer to the Pacific Ocean it was exciting. We ended up in Oregon, a beautiful state and one I considered staying in."

"The biggest problem of this trip was once we arrived in the West we did not look forward to the drive back, but knew it had to be done. The trip turned out great and was a one chance thing I'm glad I got to do. We were lucky that the trip was problem free and was a tremendous learning and maturing experience."

Without doing any type of calculations, we can see the story has a very short ending consisting of just over five lines. This would be an indication the person has made up this story. When you do the math you find the "Before the Incident" segment, which consists of 11.5 lines, equals 31.3% of the story. The "During the Incident" segment, which has 20 lines, equals 54.5% of the story. The "After the Incident" segment, which is comprised of 5.2 lines, equals 14.2% of the story. This falls short of the 25% we expect to see in the "After the Incident" segment. To figure out the percentages, multiply the number of lines per segment by 100. Then divide that number by the total number of lines in the statement. For example, if a segment contained a total of 16.5 lines, the calculation would be 16.5 x 100 = 1,650. If there are a total of 30 lines in the statement, you would divide 1,650 by 30 and get 55 or 55%.

The person who wrote this story about traveling across the country admitted that he made it up. It was something he always wanted to do but he never got the chance to do it. Because this was something he had thought about many times, he was able to give a statement that sounds believable. When you analyze the language, there are very few indications of deception. However, when you look at the story breakdown you can see it has a very short ending. There may have been many days in which he contemplated taking this trip out West. However, he probably never thought about making the trip back home. Therefore, he did not have much information to share in the "After the Incident" segment.

Here is a story about an alleged kidnapping and robbery. Again, I have broken down the story into the three segments.

"This morning around 9:00 a.m., I walked to the grocery store on 10th street to buy a few items. I was at the store for only a few minutes. As I was walking back home this guy approached me and asked me for some money. I told him I did not have any money."

"He then pulls out a gun and points it at me pushing me towards the car. He forced me to get in the back of the car. He then got in with me. He told the driver to move out. I asked him what he wanted and he told me to keep quiet. He grabbed my purse and started going through it. He took my money out of my purse and gave me my purse back. We drove around for maybe 10 minutes and then he told the driver to stop the car. Once he stopped the car he told me to get out and not to call the police or he would come back and shoot me."

"I got out of the car and walked home. When I got home I called the police."

We can clearly see this statement has a very short ending consisting only two sentences. This would be an indication the person is making up the story about being kidnapped and robbed. This story can be broken down into the follow percentages: Before = 30.6%, During = 61.2%, After = 8.2%.

We also see deception when we look at the subject's language. She wrote, "As I was walking back home this guy approached me." Although the word *this* identifies a specific guy, it also shows closeness. We would not expect the victim to associate with the guy robbing her. A better statement would have been to state, "a guy approached me." She goes on to say, "He then pulls out a gun and points it at me pushing me towards the car." This entire sentence is in the present tense. We see this with the words *pulls*, *points* and *pushing*. Had she been recalling this story from memory, she would have stated, "He pulled out a gun and pointed it at me and pushed me towards a car." She refers to the car as "the car" and not "a car." This indicates she either recognizes the car or she is making up the story. She tells us that "he grabbed my purse and started going through it." The word *started* means the act was interrupted and perhaps never completed. Was there a time when he stopped and then resumed looking through her purse? A more definite statement would be to say, "He went through my purse." The woman eventually confessed she made up the story about being kidnapped.

As you examine the story breakdown, here are the percentages to keep in mind.

Segments	Truthful Story	Deceptive Story
Before	25%	35%
During	50%	50%
After	25%	15%

Any significant deviation from this formula is an indication of deception. For example, a story may have a proper ending consisting of about 25% of the entire story. However, if the story has a short beginning (15%) or it has a very big beginning (50%) this would signify the person is making up the story.

If you want to detect deception, look at the story breakdown. As you are reading the story, draw a line in the margin separating the "Before," "During" and "After Incident" segments. This will help you to see if the story is balanced. Many deceptive stories will have a very short ending. However, any substantial departure from the 25 - 50 - 25 formula is an indication that the story is a fabrication.

We must remember that if a person experiences a traumatic event, immediately following the incident the person may not want to talk about what happened. Therefore, their statement may have a significant beginning and a significant ending. However, he or she may talk very little about the incident. While the story breakdown may indicate deception their actions and mannerisms should show you they traumatized and most likely being truthful.

Also, if we are accounting for a person's whereabouts during a particular day, we may ask him to tell us what he did from the time he woke up to the time he went to sleep. When analyzing his statement we will not be able to use the story breakdown. His story will not contain the three segments since there was no incident.

CHAPTER 19

Punctuation

In a written statement, the rules of grammar require that we place some form of punctuation at the end of the sentence. This can be a period, exclamation point or a question mark depending on the type of sentence. We use a period to end a sentence that makes a statement. The writer may continue on writing about the same subject matter, but when he is finished with one specific thought he will indicate this with a period. When the subject does not place a period or any other type of punctuation at the end of a sentence it is an indication of conflict at that point in his story. Although the writer has intentionally stopped writing about this one specific thought, he may have more information that he purposefully withheld. Because he is contemplating whether or not he should write down more information, he unknowingly forgets to end the sentence with a period. No period at the end of a sentence means the writer probably has more information to share.

In chapters two and four, we looked at the statement given by a man who said he accidentally let his car roll over a cliff with his wife still in the car. We saw various signs of deception in his language which included two fragmented sentences which appeared at the end of his statement.

"This is a tragic accident that how or why it happened. I never wanted to let her go and don't how this happened"

In both sentences, he stops short of stating that he did not know how this happened. When we look at the last sentence of his statement we see he did not end it with a period. This tells us he probably has more information to share but he chose to withhold it. Most likely this additional information is that he knows this was not an accident.

In the JonBenet Ramsey murder, a three page ransom note was left at the Ramsey's residence. The writer signed the ransom note "Victory!"[1] and below that word wrote the letters "S.B.T.C."[2] There has been much speculation on what these letters stand for. Some leading theories as to their meaning are "So Be The Case" "Saved By The Cross" and "Shall Be The Conqueror." For all I know, it could mean "Slow Boat To China!" Unfortunately, this acronym has not been matched to anyone. When we look at the original writing we see the writer did not place a period after the letter "C." The first three letters all have a period but the writer forgot to put a period after the last letter. This would indicate that even though the writer was ending this ransom note, he had more information to share but purposefully withheld it. Because he was thinking about something else, most likely in regards to JonBenet, it caused him to forget to place a period after the letter "C."

An exclamation point is used at the end of a sentence to indicate strong feelings or inject a high volume. When we end a sentence with a period, the rules of grammar require we only use one period. However, a writer is not limited in how many exclamations points he can place at the end of a sentence. When a person uses several exclamation points, he is portraying a high intensity of emotion. How many exclamation points a person uses can sometimes reveal additional information.

I once was asked to analyze a note that was found in a clothing store. The writer stated she was a 12-year-old girl who had been kidnapped by a "white old man." The police wanted to know if the note was legitimate and what information did the note reveal. I noticed the writer had used a lot of exclamation points. When I examined them I found the following exclamation points listed in the order they were written:

"Help me!"
"Please!"
"This is not a joke!"
"I am not aware of where he is hiding me!"
"My name is Christie Burlow I am 12 years old!!!"
"HELP ME!!!!!!"

We see that four times the writer used one exclamation point. This is the number most people would probably use. One exclamation point is usually all the emphasis that is needed. At the end of the note, the writer used six exclamation points. While this seems excessive it could be justified because of the plea for help and because the words *HELP ME* are capitalized and consist of six letters. The problem is with the fifth sentence, "My name is Christie Burlow I am 12 years old!!!" The writer uses three exclamation points which deviate from the one he or she had been using. More emphasis is placed on this sentence than the first pleas of "Help me!" and "Please!" What is odd is that the writer is placing a lot of emphasis on the victim being twelve years old. This indicates that someone other than the victim wrote this note. To the writer, it is serious and shocking that this kidnapped victim is only twelve years old. We sometimes express more sympathy for kids who have been victimized than we do for adults. If the hostage wrote this note, she probably would not make a big deal about the fact she is twelve. Her age does not matter. The emphasis should not be on her age but on the fact she needs help. The three exclamation points show us from what point of view this note was written.

There were other signs this note was bogus. The writer wrote, "Everywhere I go I drop notes." The writer is acting as if she is free to walk around town. A better statement would have been, "Everywhere he takes me I drop notes." The note said, "I am not aware of where he is hiding me." A better and stronger statement would be, "I don't know where he is hiding me." The note also lacked details. The kidnapper was only described as a "white old man." A twelve-year-old should be able to give a better description of her abductor. The writer also had a change in language in describing the license plate of the vehicle driven by her abductor. One time she referred it as a "license tag" and then later called it a "car tag." The police never found a victim or the writer and concluded the note was a fake.

We see an overuse of the exclamation point in an email that a boyfriend sent to his girlfriend. The boyfriend was allegedly going through some tough times and wanted to take a break from their relationship. Therefore, he sent his girlfriend the following email:

"Jill, I am really sorry! I never wanted to hurt you! I am sorry the way things worked out! I am sure we will see each other again! I really hope you will be all right and everything will be ok! Steve"

This short note is comprised of five sentences and every sentence ends with an exclamation point. Not once does the writer use a period. The exclamation point used in the first sentence may be justified to emphasize his claim of being sorry. However, the use of an exclamation point to intensify his statement that they may see each other again in the future doesn't seem right. The fact he used an exclamation point to end every sentence indicates he may not be sincere in what he is saying. This is validated in that three times he used the word *really* to add emphasis to his feelings. The word *really* is a word that indicates untruthfulness. Although he was leading her to believe they would get back together after a short break, his language and punctuation marks indicate he does not want to continue the relationship.

If you want to detect deception, look at the punctuation in a written statement. Many times a missing period goes unnoticed especially if the subject's handwriting is difficult to read. As you analyze a written statement you should concentrate on one sentence at a time. Look to see what the sentence is telling you including the punctuation. A missing period may indicate the writer is withholding information. Excessive or improper use of the exclamation point may also provide you with some additional information.

Part 3

The Actions of a Liar

Nonverbal Communication

Nonverbal Communication

In addition to vocalizing our thoughts, we also communicate with others through our body language. Our nonverbal communication can sometimes speak just as loud as our words. Research shows that approximately 90 percent of our communication is nonverbal. Nonverbal communication includes posture, facial expressions, eye contact, hand movements, and leg movements. Your nonverbal signals express your emotional state. Your posture, whether walking, standing, or sitting can indicate if you are confident, relaxed, bored, or defensive. Facial expressions can show if you are happy, surprised, fearful, or disgusted without ever saying a word. Your eyes can reveal several things including if you are happy, concerned, tense or scared. Hand and leg movements can communicate nervousness, indecisiveness, and defensiveness.

Although nonverbal gestures primarily reveal emotions, they can also show if a person is being deceptive. The reason these nonverbal cues can show deception is because when a person knowingly tells a lie it creates some degree of stress. This stress will usually surface in the form of a body movement. This is similar to the principles that govern a polygraph test. A polygraph will measure a person's heart rate, respiratory rate, blood pressure, and perspiration. When abnormal changes occur in these areas it is a sign the person is tense. Even though the subject may claim he didn't do it, the polygraph is detecting stress which indicates he may be lying. While you cannot detect someone's heart rate just by looking at them, there are recognizable nonverbal signals which may indicate a person is stressed and possibly being untruthful.

The latest trend in nonverbal communication is micro-expressions. Micro-expressions are involuntary facial expressions caused by emotions. These tiny expressions can occur as fast as 1/15 of a second. While people may be able to fake some facial expressions it is very difficult to control micro-expressions. Micro-expressions can reveal if a person is being truthful or deceptive. You may have seen the show *Lie To Me* which uses micro-expressions as it's premise for detecting deception. There are over one hundred nonverbal gestures that people may use. Therefore, I have selected the most common signs that indicate deception and I have broken down these gestures into three categories: hand movements, eye movements, and leg movements.

CHAPTER 20

Hand Movements

One of the most noticeable parts of the body that can show if a person is being deceptive is the hands. We often say that some people like to talk with their hands. It seems like every word that comes out of their mouth is illustrated with a hand movement. The truth is everyone uses their hands when communicating. While some people may not be so animated with their hands they are still displaying subtle gestures that can show if they are being truthful.

When people lie they will sometimes bring their hand to their mouth. They unknowingly perform this gesture because they know the words they are speaking are not true. By covering their mouth, they are attempting to mask what they just said. You sometimes see clear examples of this with children. When a child tells a lie he may immediately cup his hand over his mouth. He is reacting to the fact he knows what he said is untrue. He may be thinking he should not have said that since he was raised to tell the truth. By placing his hand over his mouth, he is making sure he does not tell any more lies.

Once we grow out of childhood we know that slapping our hand over our mouth after giving a deceptive answer is an obvious sign we are not telling the truth. However, for some deceptive people it is hard to fight this almost instinctual reaction of bringing a hand towards their face. Instead of cupping a hand over their mouth they will disguise this move by giving a fake cough. Some deceptive people may not cover their mouth but will touch their lips with their fingers. Others may not stop at their mouth but will rub their nose or scratch their cheek. People who are better at fighting this urge of raising their hand may stop short of their mouth and touch their chin or rub their throat. They want to touch their mouth but they know this action will betray them so they touch an area near the mouth. These are all signs the person may be trying to cover up his words because he knows they are not true.

Bringing a hand to the mouth
indicates the person may not be telling the truth.

Sometimes when people tell a lie their internal stress will cause a tingling sensation in the tissues around the neck. They may begin to perspire in this area causing them to do a number of things with their hands. Using their index finger they may scratch behind their ear or scratch the side of their neck. Some people may gently rub the back of their neck or stroke the back of their head with their hand. Rubbing the back of the neck can also be a sign of frustration. The person may be upset and sees the interviewer as being a "pain in the neck." For some liars, their neck may begin to heat up when they give a deceptive answer. In an effort to cool down, they may employ what is known as the "collar pull." They may tug on their shirt collar with one hand pulling their collar away from their neck. They are trying to open up a gap so air can circulate around their neck providing them with some relief. Generally these movements will only last for a few seconds and then they will move their hand away from their neck.

Rubbing the eyes could be a sign the person has just given a deceptive answer. When a person rubs his eyes he is no longer looking at the interviewer. This could be his way of breaking eye contact. He knows what he said or is about to say is untrue. Since he cannot look the interviewer in the eyes and tell a lie, he rubs his eyes while answering a question or immediately after giving an answer.

There are also several things a person may do with his hands which indicate he is nervous and perhaps apprehensive in giving truthful answers. His nervousness may be a sign he is anxious to stop answering questions. He may withhold information only giving enough of an answer to satisfy the interviewer. One of these signs is the "finger tap." A person may tap his finger or fingers on the table, on an armrest or perhaps on his thigh. Any sign of tapping shows the person is uncomfortable and tense. Similar signs of nervousness are when the person twiddles his thumbs or rubs his hands. When some people tell a lie their hands become sweaty causing them to play with their hands.

Some people will fiddle with objects when they are feeling uneasy. They may reach into their pocket and jingle their change or they may play with their car keys. Some may fidget with a pen or pencil twirling it in their fingers or tapping it on the table. Others may do the same thing with other objects such as a cigarette.

When some people become nervous they will bite their fingernails. While there are many people who have a habit of biting their nails, most people only do this when life becomes stressful. Being deceptive may be the stress that is causing them to bite their nails. This nonverbal cue may also be associated with bringing the hand to the mouth. Instead of placing their hand over their mouth, they attempt to mask this action by biting their nails.

The hands can also show if a person is tense. Some deceptive people will unknowingly curl their fingers into a tight ball making a fist with their hand. They may also grip the armrest of their chair as if they were sitting in the dentist chair. This type of person may be stressed because he has information he does not want to share with the interviewer. He is afraid the interviewer may ask him questions he does not want to answer. The tension displayed in his hands is his way of showing resistance.

The hands can reveal if a person is stalling for time. Some people may remove their glasses to clean them. Generally, they will look down and use their shirt or a tissue to clean the lens. This type of person believes he is not expected to answer any questions while he is performing this simple task. He may be using this pause to think about how he should answer the question. He may also use this technique to break eye contact with the interviewer. Since he has removed his glasses, he cannot see clearly and therefore no longer has direct eye contact.

Another stall tactic sometimes used by deceptive people is to wind their watch. Their watch may be keeping perfect time but they feel the need to look at their watch and wind it or play with it. Again, this allows them to break eye contact and buys them time to ponder their answer. They may also be looking at their watch and thinking, "Is it time for me to go?"

Some people will begin to groom themselves when the questions become stressful. They may take their hand and run it though their hair making sure their hair is in place. This person may be thinking that if he looks good then his answers will look good. He may also begin to pick lint from his clothes or adjust his clothing in an effort to make sure he looks neat. These nonverbal gestures may also be used as a stall tactic.

Lastly, the hands, or more precisely the arms, can show if a person is closed off and not open to what the interviewer is saying. When we feel threatened a natural response is to hide behind a barrier. This is why children will sometimes stand behind a parent if they feel threatened by what is in front of them. If a person is standing or sitting with his arms crossed, he is unconsciously creating a barrier between himself and the interviewer. Through this nonverbal gesture he is telling the interviewer he is not interested in what he is saying or asking. If his arms are uncrossed, this is an indication he is open to the conversation.

Despite the smile his crossed arms indicate he is closed-off.

If you want to detect deception by observing nonverbal cues, an interviewer must first establish the interviewee's normal body movements. This should be done at the beginning of the interview when the subject is being asked questions he should answer truthfully. Personal data questions about the person's name, address, and telephone number should not be stressful to the subject. Once you have established a baseline for the person you then look for the abnormal movements. When the hand comes towards the mouth this could be a sign the person has just told a lie. You should ask him to repeat his answer. Some people will find it difficult to tell a lie a second time. At this point in the interview, he may choose to give you a truthful answer. If the person rubs a part of his body such as the back of his neck or ear, this could be an indication he is under some stress. You will want to find out what is causing the stress. If the person's hands indicate he is nervous or tense, you will need to discover the reason for his anxiety. If a person crosses his arms, he is signifying he is closed off. At this point in the interview, he may start to give deceptive answers. Handing him something such as a document or a pen forces him to uncross his arms. By removing his barrier, he may become more cooperative. You can learn a lot about a person by watching what he or she does with their hands.

CHAPTER 21

Eye Movements

When we are engaged in a conversation most of our attention is drawn to the person's eyes. It has been said the eyes are the window to the soul. The eyes can reveal a person's true thoughts. This is why many of our sayings reference the eyes; "He gave me the evil eye," "She has bedroom eyes," "He has shifty eyes," "If looks could kill." How much eye contact a person makes, which direction a person looks, and the size of his pupils can show if he is being deceptive, if he is tense, relaxed, or if he is not interested in the conversation.

In most parts of the world, it is customary and polite to maintain some degree of eye contact when speaking with someone. This shows the person you are interested in what he is saying. Staring at a person during a conversation is abnormal. Most people will briefly look away and then reacquire eye contact. If a person constantly looks away while giving an answer there is a good chance he is being deceptive. This type of person cannot look you in the eyes and lie. If the person looks away for a prolonged period of time, it is an indication he is not interested in the conversation and wants to end the discussion.

The person who closes his eyes while answering a question may not be completely forthright. This is similar to looking away while giving an answer. The person knows he should maintain eye contact. Therefore, he will not turn his head and look away. However, he cannot look at you and lie. So, he simply closes his eyes while talking. This may also be a sign he is rejecting what you are saying.

When engaged in a conversation it is natural to occasionally break eye contact and look away. Therefore, something is amiss if a person maintains prolonged eye contact. This could be his way of letting you know he is upset. His disappointment should be obvious. It could also be the subject is being deceptive. He knows if he looks away while answering a question or if he has low eye contact this could be interpreted as a sign he is lying. In order to make his answers sound believable, he makes sure he is looking at you. Chances are he will overcompensate and make too much eye contact. He may do this without blinking since he is forcing himself to maintain eye contact.

On average, people blink about 10 to 20 times per minute. This is a normal action that helps to lubricate the eyes. People who are tense and telling a lie may have an increase in their blink rate that is four times that of a truthful person. The stress placed on a deceptive person's body may cause his eyes to dry. The person then blinks excessively in an effort to lubricate his eyes. For some deceptive people, an increase blink rate is their way of shutting out the interviewer. By momentarily closing their eyes, they do not see the person thus providing them with some relief. For some people, just before they tell a lie their eyes will begin to flutter. This occurs because their mind is racing as they search for a deceptive answer.

When a right-handed person looks up and to his left he is using the part of his brain where he stores images. If you asked a person the color of his first car, he most likely will look up and to his left as he visualizes the first vehicle he owned. When answering a question, a person who looks up and to his left is most likely drawing his answer from memory and is probably being truthful.

If you asked a person to visualize a pink elephant, he would probably look up and to his right. This is because he is not selecting this image from his memory. Instead, he is creating this image in his mind. A person who looks in this direction while answering a question may be making up his answer. He is relying on his creativity and not his memory to form his response.

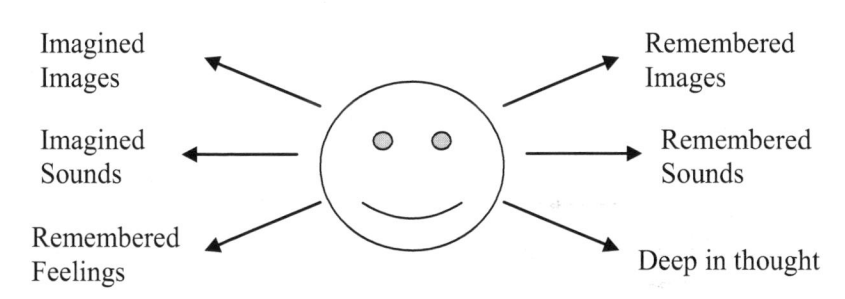

Imagined Images	←	Remembered Images →
Imagined Sounds ←	👀	→ Remembered Sounds
Remembered Feelings ←	⌣	→ Deep in thought

Visual cues for a right-handed person

As the chart above indicates, when a person looks to his lateral right or lateral left this involves auditory processing. If you asked a person to think of his favorite song, a truthful person will most likely look to his left as he recalls what the tune sounds like. A person who looks down and to the right is recalling feelings whether emotional or measurable by touch. A person who looks down and to his left may be talking to himself. This will not be a verbal conversation but he will be deep in thought. The direction one looks would be the opposite for a left-handed person.

A person who looks up and to the right
may be drawing his story from his imagination.

    The eyes can also provide information through pupil dilation. Our pupils will dilate or constrict depending on how much light is around us. This process allows us to have optimal vision. A person's pupils will also change depending on his emotional state. When a person is experiencing pleasure, his pupils will usually be dilated (larger in size). This is why some poker players wear dark sun glasses. Enlarged pupils could reveal they are holding a good hand. A truthful person who has nothing to hide may have dilated or normal size pupils. The converse is those individuals who have constricted pupils (smaller in size). If the subject is being interrogated with a bright light in his face, this may explain why his pupils are constricted. However, under normal lighting conditions a person with constricted pupils is unknowingly revealing he is under some stress. This could be a sign he does not like the person who is conducting the interview or he does not like the questions he is being asked. It could also be a sign he is giving deceptive answers.

If you want to detect deception, watch what a person does with his eyes. If he does not maintain eye contact or looks away while giving an answer, this could be a sign he is not being truthful. He may not be able to look you in the eyes and tell you a lie. If a person does not break eye contact, he may be trying too hard to convince you he is telling the truth. His intensive look is a sign he is lying. If one looks up and to his right while thinking about his response, this is an indication he is giving a fabricated the story. Remember this is based on the fact the person is right-handed. If the subject is a southpaw, then deception would come when he looks up and to his left. An easy nonverbal cue to observe is excessive blinking. This indicates the person is tense. This tension may arise from the fact the person is being dishonest. The hardest nonverbal sign to utilize which involves the eyes is pupil dilation. The further away the subject is from you the more difficult it is to see his pupils. Dilated pupils may mean the person is relaxed and giving you truthful answers. Constricted pupils indicate the person is under some stress which may have been caused by the person's deception.

CHAPTER 22

Leg Movements

Because the nonverbal techniques have been around for a while, most liars are familiar with some of the gestures that can show they are being deceptive. Therefore, they will try and control their facial expressions, hand, and eye movements when giving a false answer. However, the anxiety caused from lying may show up in the lower half of the body. One of the areas that people often overlook is the legs and feet. When a person is drawn to another person he will face that person when engaging in a conversation. If a person is looking to his left while talking to a friend seated to his right he is not giving his friend his undivided attention. In addition to eye contact, our feet will also point in the direction to which we have an attraction. You can use this technique when you meet someone of the opposite sex at a social function. You may be having a pleasant conversation with this person. He or she may be maintaining eye contact with you, smiling and laughing at your jokes. However, if you look down and see that their feet are pointed towards someone else, then it is time for you to move on! In an interview setting, if the subject is not pointing his feet at the interviewer, this could be a sign he is not interested in answering the questions being asked of him. Therefore, he may be giving deceptive answers.

Another sign that a person may be apprehensive and does not want to participate in the interview is when he draws his legs back under his chair. This is an indication he is trying to pull away from the interviewer. This nonverbal gesture may be accompanied by the person leaning his body back and away from the interviewer. This is an attempt to create some distance between himself and the interviewer. This negative reaction may have something to do with what the interviewer just said or just asked. A person who is relaxed and giving truthful answers will usually have his feet in front of him. He will sit upright and may even lean towards the interviewer.

When a person crosses his legs he is unconsciously creating a barrier between himself and the person he is talking to. Some people will do this because it helps them to relax and feel comfortable. They may cup their hands over their knee or grab their ankle with one hand while their legs are crossed. This positioning gives them something to do with their hands so they don't appear to be fidgeting. This type of person could be giving truthful answers. This is his way of dealing with the stress brought on, not by his deceptive answers, but by the authority figure asking the questions. For others though, this action creates an invisible wall signaling the person is becoming defensive. Often, the person will cross his arms at the same time creating a double barrier. This gesture may come at a point in the interview when the person decides to give a deceptive answer.

A sign of tension is when a man is seated with his feet and knees together. Most men who are relaxed will sit with their legs slightly spread apart. Bringing the feet and knees together is similar to making a fist with the hands. The higher the anxiety level the tighter he will press his feet and knees together. This nonverbal gesture may not apply to women as some women will normally sit with their knees together and their feet off to one side of their body.

Whether standing or sitting, a liar does not always keep his feet flat on the ground. He may consciously control his facial expressions and hand movements, but a deceptive person is usually unaware of what he is doing with is feet. He may shift from foot to foot, shuffle his feet, or tap his foot. These signs of nervousness are usually associated with the "flight instinct." When a person gets into an uncomfortable circumstance he naturally wants to back out of the situation. In the case of an interview, he wants to leave so he does not have to answer any questions.

If you want to detect deception, look to see what the person is doing with his legs. If his feet are not pointed at you, then he may not be interested in what you are saying. Crossing his legs, placing his feet under his chair, leaning back, and keeping his feet together are signs he is nervous and tense and does not want to be answering your questions. The key is to notice when he makes these nonverbal gestures. These cues may come at a point in the interview when the subject has just told a lie or has withheld information.

Part 4

The Handwriting of a Liar

Handwriting Styles

Handwriting Styles

Just as everyone has their own personal dictionary, everyone also has their own writing style. No two people have the exact same handwriting. One reason for this is that everyone has a slightly different build. The structural differences in our fingers, hands and grip create a unique handwriting that is not duplicated by anyone else. A person's personality also plays a role in shaping one's handwriting. There are numerous traits such as being confident, persistent, ambitious, aggressive, and violent, that can influence how a person writes.

Handwriting is brain writing. While your conscious mind decides what to write your subconscious mind determines how you will write. There are numerous characteristics such as the size of the letters, how much pressure is applied to the paper, the spacing of the words, and the slant of the letters that can reveal a person's personality. Look at the following two handwriting samples. Which person would you consider to be an extrovert and which one is an introvert?

I will see you tonight.

I will see you tonight.

People who write very large are usually more outgoing. Their assertive personality jumps off the page with the size of their writing. The bigger the letters the more gregarious this person will be. Conversely, a person who has very small handwriting is typically an introvert. His compact writing style indicates he is detailed oriented and likes to keep to himself.

Graphology, sometimes referred to as handwriting analysis, is the study of a person's handwriting in an effort to develop a personality profile of the writer. It has its origins in ancient history. Over 2,000 years ago, the Chinese developed a correlation between a person's handwriting and personality traits. Some Roman Emperors evaluated the aptitude of his associates by analyzing their handwriting. Handwriting analysis has been used for a long time in Europe as an assessment tool in hiring a person for a job. If the applicant's handwriting indicates he is a procrastinator, prone to violence, or a potential thief the employer will probably not offer him a job.

Not only can handwriting provide insight into a person's character but a person's writing style can also show if he is being deceptive. Because the person knows what he is writing is not the truth, this will cause him to unknowingly alter his writing style. This is more prominent when a person is writing in cursive versus printing. Let's examine some ways in which a person's handwriting can reveal if he is being deceptive.

CHAPTER 23

Handwriting Traits

The Letter O

One of the easiest ways to tell if a person is being deceptive is to look at how he writes the letter *o*. Most people will write the letter *o* forming a circle that has no additional lines or loops inside the oval. This writing style is an indication the person is being honest and candid. When a loop appears inside the *o* this is a sign the person is secretive.

| An honest *o* | Left side loop | Right side loop |

When the loop is on the left side this indicates the person is keeping a secret from himself. He is lying to himself because he is in self-denial. There is something major going on in his life that he is avoiding. When the loop is to the right this represents he is keeping secrets from others. This may be in an effort to save face. This person may believe his lies thus he finds it easy to tell a lie. We see the right hand loop in the handwriting of Phillip Garrido. On June 10, 1991, Garrido kidnapped 11-year-old Jaycee Lee Dugard from a school bus stop near her home in South Lake Tahoe, California. Although the police received over

1,000 leads they could not locate Dugard and did not know who abducted her. In 2009, it was discovered that 29-year-old Jaycee Dugard was living in a makeshift shed behind Phillip Garrido's home. The authorities believe Garrido kept Dugard hidden for 18 years. She had given birth to two daughters who were fathered by Garrido. Garrido and his wife Nancy were arrested and charged with kidnapping and false imprisonment. Dugard and her children were reunited with her family.

In all respects my life has changed. Of course that is because I wanted to, knowing this is my chance to get my life in line.

Phillip Garrido consistently places a loop in the right side of the letter *o*.

The biggest indication that a person is a liar is the double inner loop within the letter *o*. This will show up as a loop on the left and right side. This person may lie or simply withhold the truth. If these two loops overlap creating an inner circle, this indicates the person is a pathological lair. His lying is uncontrollable. He will lie even if there is nothing to be gained from it. The more convoluted the ovals appear the greater the chance the person is being deceptive.

Double inner loops

Instead of placing a loop within the letter *o* some deceptive people may draw a line inside the oval. Studies have shown that a high percentage of chronic liars will have this stab stroke. This trait is not limited to the letter *o* but may also appear within the ovals of the letters *a*, *b*, *d*, *g* and *q*. One line in an oval does not mean the person is a liar. However, if this stroke appears often in their handwriting it is a strong indication the person is not to be trusted.

I love you

The stab marks in the letter *o* indicate the writer may not be sincere.

Another sign a person is being evasive is when the writer retraces a letter. While this can occur with any letter it usually appears in the letter *o* as well as the other letters that contain an oval. The writer may circle the letter *o* twice causing it to have a bold look. This indicates he may have mentally paused to think about what to write. As he pondered his statement his pen kept moving retracing the letter.

I did not take the money

The letter *o* in this sentence has been retraced.

If the story is coming from memory, it should flow smoothly. The writer should not have to pause and contemplate what he is going to write down. Hesitation seen in the form of retracing indicates the writer may have decided to withhold some information. What he has written down using the retraced letters may be a lie.

In Statement Analysis, the shortest sentence is the best sentence. Extra words give us extra information. The same principle applies to how a person writes the letter *o*. When the writer adds additional strokes such as double loops, stab marks or retracing, the greater the chance he is lying.

Open Ovals

Ovals can be found in the letters, *a, b, d, g, o, p* and *q*. Ovals symbolize how a person communicates. Clean ovals that have no additional marks indicate the writer is candid in his communication. The more an oval becomes distorted with additional lines and loops, the more deceitful the writer will be. When writing a letter with an oval some people will fail to make a complete circle and will leave an open area within the oval. These are referred to as "open ovals." When the opening appears at the top of the letter, this signifies the writer is talkative and may like to gossip. This person may not be able to keep a secret.

When the opening appears at the bottom of the oval, this is referred to as the "embezzler's script." Many thieves possess this handwriting trait. It is also associated with people who commit heinous crimes and are so dishonest they lie without conscience. We see the "embezzler's script" in the handwriting of serial killer Jeffrey Dahmer who killed 17 men and boys.

again. This is why, Judge Gardner, I am requesting from you, a sentence modification. So that I may be allowed to continue my life as a productive member of our society.

*Respectfully Yours,
Jeff Dahmer*

The handwriting of serial killer Jeffrey Dahmer

In Dahmer's handwriting, the open oval often appears at the bottom of letter *a*. It even shows up in his name. Open ovals that are located at the bottom of the letter are a sign the writer is corrupt and deceitful.

Word Spacing

How much space a person places between his words can provide insight into one's personality. Most people write with average spacing. One word follows another as if the person was speaking. The words in this book are evenly spaced making it easy to read. When people deviate from this norm their handwriting shows us their emotional status. When a person writes with a narrow spacing between his words this signifies the person is insecure. He likes to be around other people for the social contact. When a person has wide gaps between his words this indicates he is an introvert. He isolates himself so he can avoid dealing with people. Look at the wide spaces in the following handwriting:

> I recently received a page from the <u>Washington Post</u>, June 19, 2008, page A9. This comprises a full-page, full-color advertisement that features my cabin, which is being exhibited publicly at something called a "Newseum". The page in question is attached hereto as Exhibit A. Information about the "Newseum" is provided in Exhibit B.
> Since the advertisement states that the cabin is "FROM FBI VAULT",

    This is the handwriting of Ted Kaczynski also known as the "Unabomber" (University and Airline Bomber). For nearly 20 years, Kaczynski sent bombs through the mail to protest technology because it was infringing on his lifestyle. When he was arrested in April 1996, it was discovered that for 25 years he had been living in a remote cabin outside of Lincoln, Montana. The cabin was only 10-by-12 foot in size and contained no electricity or running water. Kaczynski's lifestyle as a recluse can been seen in the wide spacing found in his handwriting.

    Deception may be present when a person has wide spacing at a certain point in his writing. When a person pauses while speaking it often means he is thinking about what to say. He may decide to withhold some information or he may choose to tell a lie at this point in his story. An occasional wide spacing in handwriting indicates a mental pause. The person will continue to move his hand to the right as he thinks about what to write.

However, his pen will not touch the paper until he has decided what to write. This hesitation will create a larger gap between two words.

Went to the store
The wide spacing between the words *to* and *the* indicates the writer may not have gone to the store.

This unintentional spacing is a sign the writer may have stopped drawing his story from memory and is now being creative in his writing. Lying requires extra thinking. There is a good chance the information that follows a single wide space may not be truthful.

Line Slope

When we were in kindergarten we practiced our writing skills on lined paper that had widely spaced lines with a dotted line in between the solid lines. All of these lines helped us to write the correct letter formation, uniform letter size, and uniform slant. As we got older, the dotted lines disappeared from the writing paper. The lines remained wide ruled giving us plenty of room to write the letters. As high school students, the paper became medium ruled or college ruled with a smaller space between the lines allowing for more lines on the paper.

The lines on a paper not only assist us in writing the correct height and width of the letters, but they also help us to write in a straight line. Even if a person has sloppy handwriting he will usually write parallel lines across the page because his hand is following the lines on the paper. When a person is given a blank sheet of paper he is not bound by any lines. He is free to write any way he chooses. He may write some letters that are exceptionally tall because he has no lines that tell him the letter should only be a certain height. He may find that his writing starts to slope upwards or downwards because again he has no lines on the paper to guide him across the page.

When a person is writing a deceptive statement the entire statement will usually not be false. In fact, the majority of the statement may be true. This allows a deceptive person to write most of his statement without any hesitation. He can freely guide the pen or pencil across the paper in a straight line. However, when he gets to the point in his story where he is writing a lie, his handwriting may begin to drift upwards or downwards. Because he is thinking about what he should or should not write, he is not looking to see if he is writing in a straight line. He unknowingly begins to write his lines with an upward or downward slant. This sloping may only occur in a couple of words and then the writer will be back on track writing in a straight line. This "rollercoaster" effect should be easily seen if you are looking for it.

After I left the club I went to Bob's house

Here is a sentence that drifts upwards and then downwards.

The key in examining the line slope is to establish the normal writing slope for the person and then look for any abnormal slants. When the entire statement is written with a rising slope the writer is generally optimistic and energetic. Those who continually write in a downward slant are usually seen as being pessimistic and lacking self confidence. However, when the slope changes at certain points within the statement this indicates the person may be writing an untruth.

The Felon's Claw

The felon's claw can be found mainly in the lower case letters *g*, *y* and *z*. This trait may also appear in the capital letters *A*, *G*, *H* and *J*. It has been said that 80 percent of prison inmates possess this trait thus giving this attribute its name. The felon's claw is created when a person makes a straight down-stroke that turns into a claw or hook. Usually the stroke creating the claw will veer up and towards the left. The claw could also appear at the end of the downward stroke in the form of a sickle.

Examples of the felon's claw found in lower and upper case letters.

The felon's claw is associated with guilt. While growing up the writer was made to feel inferior. He has guilty feelings about something that happened in his life. He has carried this guilt into adulthood. He uses the hook in the felon's claw to grab a hold of and hold on to past criticisms. A person who possesses this writing trait is self-destructive. He believes he is not worthy of any good thing happening to him. Therefore, he will do things that will ruin his life. He may be mentally unbalanced but this will go unnoticed. This person will appear to be very kind and helpful.

The felon's claw is also a sign the person is seeking to harm someone. The claw in the letter is seen as a weapon. The person's sincerity is only masking his desire to stab or claw you in the back. If the claw or hook is not well formed, this person may not be physically aggressive. Instead, he will seek retribution in a more passive way. He may call his target on the phone and then hang up when the person answers. He may sign someone up for a magazine subscription the person did not order. When the claw or hook has a sharp angle this indicates the writer may be physically violent. This person is very vindictive and will lash out against anyone who infringes on his personal life. A person whose handwriting has the felon's claw should not to be trusted.

Pressure

Pressure refers to how much force is applied to the paper as a person writes his statement. Most people write with moderate pressure. Their penmanship is not too heavy or too light but dark enough for people to read. You may be able to look at the writing and tell if the person has used light or heavy pressure. The easiest way to determine if a person writes with heavy pressure is to rub your fingers along the back of the paper. If you feel an imprint, he is a heavy writer.

People who write with a light pressure are usually more sensitive and not very ambitious. They are followers and not leaders. Heavy writers have much more willpower and determination. They have an abundance of energy and may have an overbearing personality. The key to analyzing the pressure, in order to determine if the person is being truthful, is to look for consistency. When writing a lie some people will press harder on the paper. If the heavy pressure only occurs at certain areas within the statement, it may be this portion of the statement is deceptive. If the entire statement is written with heavy pressure, then the writer may just be an intense person.

If you want to detect deception, look closely at the person's handwriting. You should always have the subject write his statement on a blank sheet of paper. This will be more revealing than allowing him to use ruled paper. If you find any inconsistencies such as a line having a "rollercoaster" effect, a large space appearing between two words, or some words are written with heavier pressure, you should seek to see if the person was being deceptive at that point in his story. Pay close attention to the letter *o* and any other letters that contain an oval. If the ovals are not completely enclosed or if a loop or a line appears within the ovals the person may be withholding the truth. You should also look for the felon's claw. If the writer has this trait, he may be violent and deceptive. The general rule in handwriting analysis is to see if the deceptive trait continually appears throughout the statement.

Final Thoughts

If you want to detect deception, pay close attention to the words a person uses. Since people mean exactly what they say, the Statement Analysis techniques are very accurate. A person will always word his statement based on all his knowledge. This will cause him to reveal more information than what he realized. When telling a deceptive story the person will not have a memory to rely upon. This may cause him to use the wrong pronouns, verb tenses, articles, and time references. There may be parts of his statement that are out of order because he is not recalling things that actually happened.

Remember, when analyzing a statement you are not interpreting what the person has said. Instead, you are pointing out what the person has put into words. While I don't make it a habit of quoting cartoon characters, Homer Simpson summed it up best when he said, "It takes two to lie; one to lie and one to listen." If you are not listening to what a person is saying, you may be allowing him to get away with telling a lie. Analyzing a person's words provides you with the best opportunity to detect deception.

Although not as accurate as Statement Analysis, you should also take advantage of any nonverbal signals the subject may be displaying. It is difficult to tell a lie and not exhibit a nonverbal gesture. The hands will often be the part of the body that will tell you if a person is lying. A deceptive person may bring his hand towards his mouth or rub the back of his neck. He may cross his arms indicating he is closed off. Deception can also be detected by observing a person's eye movements. He may not be able to look you in the eye and tell a lie. He may look in the wrong direction when thinking about what to say. How a person positions his legs can show you if he is open to what you are saying or if he is tense and nervous. The key to reading nonverbal cues is to establish a baseline for the subject. Once you know what his normal movements are you then look for any abnormal movements.

If you are analyzing a written statement, you can utilize Statement Analysis as well as handwriting analysis in an effort to detect deception. Look to see how the writer has written the letter *o*. Anything other than a clean oval indicates the person may be secretive. He may be keeping a secret from himself or he may be hiding something from you. You should also examine the lines that go across the page. Are they straight and parallel to each other or does one line drift upwards or downwards? Words that are written with heavy pressure or large spacing between words are a sign that something may be amiss. Of the three methods that I have discussed, handwriting analysis offers the fewest techniques for detecting deception. However, when examining a written statement you should still utilize these techniques.

If a person is being deceptive, his words, actions, or writing style will betray him. It is nearly impossible for a person to tell a lie and not display some type of deceptive signal. Therefore, there should be plenty of signs for the attentive interviewer to see. When utilizing any of these techniques the key is to look for clusters. You want to find several things in the person's language, nonverbal cues, or handwriting that tell you he is being deceptive.

Notes

Chapter One
Words and Phrases

1. Transcript of Thomas Uzenski's testimony February 13, 2003.

2. Ibid.

3. Videotape of President William Clinton's Grand Jury testimony on August 17, 1998.

4. KSL News, KSL.com, "Search organized for missing jogger," July 19, 2004.

5. Transcript of Casey Anthony's interview conducted by the Orange County Sheriff's Office, FL on July 16, 2008.

6. Transcript of Casey Anthony's telephone call made on July 16, 2008.

7. CNNPolitics.com, "Biden on VP stakes," August 20, 2008.

8. CBSnews.com, "No plans for Obama to retake oath," January 21, 2009.

9. Festival de Cannes press conference for "An Inconvenient Truth," may 21, 2006.

10. *The Philadelphia Inquirer*, "Blagojevich breaks silence," December 20, 2008.

11. *The Brunswick News*, "NBC's Albert denies sodomy, assault charges," May 21, 1997.

12. FloridaToday.com, "Crist, Rubio duke it out in televised debate," March 29, 2010.

13. Ibid.

14. Transcript of Roger Clemens testimony before the Committee on Oversight and Government Reform, February 13, 2008.

Chapter Two
Unique Words

1. Videotape of KUSA / 9 News interview of Ted Haggard, November 1, 2006.

2. CNN.com, "Haggard to King: I'm guilty enough of so many things," January 29, 2009.

3. Ibid.

4. Ibid.

5. *Palm Beach Post News*, "Haggard still playing sex game," January 29, 2009.

6. *The Daily Reflector*, "Rice Denies Presidential Aspirations," March 13, 2005.

7. Videotape of "Dateline NBC" interview of John Connolly, 1999.

8. Transcript of Roger Clemens testimony before the Committee on Oversight and Government Reform, February 5, 2008.

9. *The Pact*, Steven Gillion, 2008, page 94.

10. Transcript of *Larry King Live*, February 8, 2007.

11. Transcript of *ESPN UpClose*, "Conversations with O.J. Simpson," part one, January 15, 1998.

12. Transcript of the 911 call made by Cindy Anthony, June 15, 2008.

13. *The Daily Reflector*, "Sorry Madoff pleads guilty to all charges," March 13, 2009.

14. CBSnews.com, "JonBenet confession under scrutiny," August 17, 2006.

15. CBS News *48 Hours Mystery*, "Scared to death," October 29, 2005.

16. Transcript of the 911 call made by Patrick Kennedy, March 1998.

17. MSNBC.msn.com, "FBI: Pizza bomber was not just a hostage," July 11, 2007.

18. Transcript of Bryant Gumbel's interview of Al Michaels on HBO, November 29, 2005.

19. *Daily Camera*, "Waiting for John Karr," August 20, 2006.

Chapter Three
Extra Words

1. Transcript, CBS News *Eye to Eye with Connie Chung*, February 10, 1994.

2. Ibid.

3. FOXnews.com, "KY Governor denies affair with nursing home owner," September 18, 2002.

4. Transcript of Ted Kennedy's statement to the police, July 19, 1969.

5. Videotape of Joshua Steiner testimony before the Senate Banking Committee, August 1994.

Chapter Four
Unusual Words and Phrases

1. Transcript of Paul Redden's interview of David Westerfield, February 4, 2002.

2. Ibid.

3. Transcript of Greta Van Susteren's interview of Joran van der Sloot, *Fox News On the Record*, March 1, 2006.

4. Transcript of the ABC News show 20/20, February 2008.

5. Transcript of Justin Barber's affidavit, August 26, 2002.

Chapter Five
Pronouns

1. *The Steven Truscott Story*, Steven Truscott and Bill Trent, 1971, page 49.

2. Ibid.

3. Ibid, page 54.

4. *The Lawyers Weekly*, "Ontario Court of Appeal acquits Truscott based on hypothetical trial," September 7, 2007.

5. Transcript of the conversation between O.J. Simpson and detective Tom Lange on June 17, 1994, Court TV Library.

6. Ibid.

7. Ibid.

8. Ibid.

9. *I Want To Tell You*, O.J. Simpson, 1995, page 11.

10. *The Milwaukee Journal*, "Just how did he get those nasty scratches?" April 8 1993.

11. Ibid.

12. Videotape of a statement made by Susan Smith on November 2, 1994.

13. Copy of Susan Smith's handwritten confession that was released on November 22, 1994.

Chapter Six
Verb Tenses

1. Transcript of Jim Lehrer's January 21, 1998 interview of President William Clinton as reported by the WashingtonPost.com, February 6, 1998.

2. Ibid.

3. Transcript of President William Clinton's address to the nation, August 17, 1998.

4. *The Seattle Times*, online article "Seen, Heard, Said," October 7, 1993.

5. CNN.com, "Landis pleads innocence over test," July 28, 2006.

6. *Yahoo News*, "Report: Lands admits doping and fingers Armstrong," May 20, 2010.

7. *The Guilty Plea*, Robert Rotenberg, July 2011, page 126.

8. ABCnews.go.com, "Missing woman's husband speaks to GMA, Part II," January 29, 2003.

9. Transcript of Ann Curry's interview of Douglas Davis on *The Today Show*, August 20, 2009.

10. Transcript of Nancy Grace's interview of Douglas Davis on *Nancy Grace*, August 24, 2009.

11. Transcript of Chief Mike Reaves interview of Nick McGuffin, June 28, 2000.

12. CNN Justice, articles.cnn.com, "Dad marries girlfriend, 17, to fulfill a wish for Haleigh," March 12, 2009.

13. Transcript of *Issues with Jane Velez-Mitchell*, October 6, 2009, in which she aired a portion of Ronald Cumming's interview on the *Today Show*.

Chapter Seven
Words and Phrases That Indicate Untruthfulness

1. *Orlando Sentinel*, "Raiders ready retreat," June 22, 1995.

2. *USA Today*, "Ohio hospital worker wins Mega Millions lottery prize," January 7, 2004.

3. NYDailyNews.com, "Game's up for Mega phony," January 9, 2004.

4. Fox News, transcript of *On The Record with Greta Van Susteren*, February 13, 2009.

5. Ibid.

6. Videotape of the BIO Channel *The Interrogators*, "No Shelter," May 2009.

7. *Ocala Star Banner*, "Sheriff tearfully denies accusations," January 27, 1995.

8. CBSnews.com, "Ex-Ill. Governor Rod Blagojevich on guilty verdict," June 27, 2011.

Chapter Eight
Pronouns

1. Transcript of Ted Kennedy's statement to the police, July 19, 1969.

2. Obtained from a copy of the three page ransom note.

Chapter Nine
Order Is Important

1. Obtained from a copy of O.J. Simpson's letter, June 1994.

Chapter Ten
Personal Dictionary

1. Videotape of *48 Hours Mystery*, "Invitation to Murder," January 2003.

2. Ibid.

3. Transcript of Michael Yarnell's statement to the police, October 2003.

4. *I Want To Tell You*, O.J. Simpson, 1995, page 13.

5. Ibid, page 25.

6. Obtained from a copy of Alfred Keefe's written statement, March 4, 1999.

7. Ibid.

Chapter Eleven
Emotions

1. *People* magazine, "I'm thankful I'm still here," October 27, 2008.

2. Transcript of Justin Barber's affidavit, August 26, 2002.

Chapter Twelve
Words and Phrases That Span Time

1. *The Daily Mail*, "Cabin girl in hiding after liaison with Fiennes on flight," February 12, 2007.

Chapter Fifteen
Did the Subject Answer the Specific Question?

1. *The Galveston Daily News*, "Jackson, Dukakis, Gore say don't use illegal drugs," November 7, 1987.

2. *Houston Chronicle*, "Drugs irrelevant to race, Bush says," May 3, 1994.

3. *The Pact*, Steven Gillion, 2008, page 94.

4. Transcript of President Mahmoud Ahmadinejad appearance at Columbia University, September 24, 2007.

5. *New York Times* – International, "Iran's President says Israel must be wiped off the map," October 26, 2005.

6. Transcript of Connie Chung's interview of Rep. Gary Condit, August 23, 2007.

7. Transcript of Roger Clemens testimony before the Committee on Oversight and Government Reform, February 13, 2008.

8. *Newsweek* magazine, July 3, 1995,

9. *Time* magazine, April 15, 1996.

10. CNN.com, "Landis pleads innocence over test," July 28, 2006.

11. *The Situation Room* with Wolf Blitzer, transcript of Rep. Anthony Weiner's interview, June 1, 2011.

Chapter Sixteen
Did the Subject Answer the Question with a Question?

1. *Time* magazine, September 6, 2004.

2. Transcript of the 911 call made by Cindy Anthony, June 15, 2008.

3. Transcript of Greta Van Susteren's interview of Joran van der Sloot, *Fox News On the Record*, March 1, 2006.

4. Ibid.

5. Ibid.

6. *ESPN Golf*, "Tiger Woods gets rid of Steve Williams," espn.go.com, July 21, 2011.

Chapter Seventeen
Crossed Out Words

1. Copy of Robert Cox's letter to the *Springfield News-Leader*, May 19, 1997.

2. Obtained from a copy of the three page ransom note.

3. Obtained from a copy of O.J. Simpson's letter, June 1994.

4. Ibid.

5. Ibid.

Chapter Nineteen
Punctuation

1. Obtained from a copy of the three page ransom note.

2. Ibid.